Politics in Postwar Japanese Society

Politics in
Postwar Japanese Society

Joji Watanuki

UNIVERSITY OF TOKYO PRESS

To my colleagues and friends at Sophia University

Publication was assisted by a grant from The Japan Foundation.

UTP Number 3031-37057-5149
ISBN 0-86008-190-7
Printed in Japan

Second printing, 1980

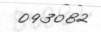

Contents

Tables

Figures

Acknowledgments

All the articles in this book, with the exception of the introduction, were written since my affiliation with the Institute of International Relations at Sophia University. I would, therefore, like to express my deep appreciation to both my colleagues and friends at Sophia for giving me stimulus and assistance in writing these articles. I would especially like to single out the following for particular thanks: President Joseph Pittau, Professor Mushakōji Kinhide, former director of the Institute, and Professor Rōyama Michio, the present director. Without their encouragement this book would not have been published. I would also like to thank the secretaries of the Institute for typing the drafts of the original papers and express my deep appreciation to Reverend David J. Wessels, Dr. Chris Kiefer, and Professor Vernon Van Dyke, who, at various stages, helped in polishing my English. I would like to thank the staff of the University of Tokyo Press, Nina Raj and Kurata Kazuhiko in particular, for their assistance and advice during the book-making process.

I would like to acknowledge the financial support received from the Japan Expo Memorial Fund for the survey conducted in Chapter 9, "Japanese Attitudes toward the Rest of the World."

The articles collected here were published earlier as listed below. I would like to thank the copyright holders for granting permission to use the material in this book.

Chapter 1   "Japan," in *The Crisis of Democracy*, by Michel J. Crozier, Samuel J. Huntington, and Joji Watanuki (New York: New York University Press, 1975). © 1975, The Trilateral Commission

Chapter 2   "Formation and Survival of Japanese Democracy after the Second World War," Institute of International Relations, Sophia University, Research Papers Series A-24, 1975. © 1975, Joji Watanuki

Chapter 3   "Japanese Politics in Flux," in *Prologue to the Future*, by James William Morley (Lexington: D. C. Heath and Co., 1974). © 1974, Japan Society, Inc.

Chapter 4   "Social Structure and Political Participation in Japan," Institute of International Relations, Research Papers Series A-9, 1973. © 1973, Joji Watanuki

Chapter 5   "Pattern of Politics in Present-day Japan," in *Party Systems and Voter Alignments*, by Seymour Martin Lipset and Stein Rokkan (New York: The Free Press, 1967). © 1967, Macmillan Publishing Co.

Chapter 6   "Intellectuals and the Structure of the 'Foreign Policy Public,'" presented at the VIIIth World Congress of Sociology, 1974. © 1974, Joji Watanuki

Chapter 7   "Nation-Building at the Edge of an Old Empire: Japan and Korea," in *Building States and Nations*, vol. 2, edited by S. N. Eisenstadt and Stein Rokkan (Beverly Hills: Sage Publications, 1973). © 1973, International Social Science Council

Chapter 8   "Some Reflections on the Typology of Nation-Building in Asia," Institute of International Relations, Sophia University, Research Papers Series A-12, 1974. © 1974, Joji Watanuki

Chapter 9   "Contemporary Japanese Perception of International Society," Institute of International Relations, Sophia University, Research Papers Series A-13, 1973, and A-16, 1974, combined and re-edited. © 1973, 1974, Joji Watanuki

Politics in Postwar Japanese Society

Introduction

The rapid social changes which have been occurring in Japan over the past several decades have given the society vast new resources for potential social development. At the same time, however, the rapidity of social change has resulted in contradictions and strains in every aspect of Japanese society—strains such as those in the political arena which were illuminated by the 1976 disclosures of large-scale bribery of Japanese government officials by the Lockheed Aircraft Corporation. The Japanese social fabric has been famous (or notorious) for being strongly identified with the past. When a nation is faced with rapid changes, this social continuity can be a source of contradiction and strain on the one hand, but on the other hand it can strengthen the society's ability to absorb change and utilize new resources.

This book is a collection of essays written over a period of nearly ten years. They variously describe the present-day Japanese political system and its historical background, explore patterns of participation within the system, and discuss political attitudes toward and relationships with the nations of Asia and the rest of the world. Underlying all these essays is the common theme of change, with its concomitant strains and potentialities, and continuity in Japanese politics and society.

Strains and Potentialities in Japanese Social Sciences

The social sciences in a free society can help the society to solve its problems through the creation and accumulation of special knowledge and skills, and can also help to maintain the freedom of such a society through their function as detached critics of the *status quo*. Japanese social sciences have built up a large world of their own; tens of thousands of professional social scientists are teaching or working in universities and other research institutions, producing more than three thousand social science publications each year (Watanuki, 1975). Postwar democracy has provided the guarantee of freedom necessary for the development of social sciences, and the expansion of higher education, besides training more and more social scientists, has produced a growing number of chairs in the universities especially for social scientists.

However, the contradictions and strains in the Japanese social sciences are serious ones. First, because social scientists can rely on a huge domestic market for both their publications and their teaching skills, they tend to be highly parochial in the sense that they care very little to contribute their knowledge and skills to the world beyond Japan. On the other hand, they have been sensitive to the achievements of the social sciences abroad and eager to know about them. Quite a few books and articles on Japanese social sciences have been published in English and other languages which can serve as media of international transmission, and large numbers of social science publications from abroad—especially those produced in North America or Western Europe—have been widely read by Japanese social scientists in their original languages and by an even broader public in Japanese translations. About 10 percent of the social science books published in Japan—roughly three hundred books—are translations from foreign—mainly Western—languages.

Second, although Japanese social scientists have built up a tradition of empirical analysis of Japanese society, there has been an incongruity between these empirical analyses and the theories and concepts learned from Western social sciences, or between "empiricists" and "theorists" among Japanese social scientists. Some theorists seem to have been too busy to do more than just follow the achievements of the social sciences in the West, and their work looks like just the textualism of the Western social sciences. On the other hand, empiricists tend to be too involved in detailed empirical analysis of the particularities of Japanese society and are often unable either to link their analyses with theories introduced from the Western social sciences or to construct their own theories based on empirical analyses of Japanese society. Lack of cross-national or cross-cultural comparative surveys and even of a comparative viewpoint tends to result in highly descriptive, detailed studies which contribute little to theoretical generalization.

A third problem for the social sciences in Japan is that of a role for themselves in policy formation. Of course contributing to policy formation is not the sole function of the social sciences. Transmission of social knowledge, facilitating our understanding of our own and other societies, and criticism of the *status quo*—all these are roles played by the social sciences in free and complex societies. However, it can be argued that it would be profitable for a society to have some social scientists who are policy-oriented and give advice on policies, on the one hand, and decision-makers who are prepared to listen to social scientists, on the other. The Japanese social sciences have begun to move in this direction, but, at least so far, only a modest start has been made. Progress has been most evident in the field of economics. For more than a decade, the Economic Planning Agency of the Japanese government has been noted for its competent "government economists," and many academic economists have been serving as members of the government's various deliberation councils. Recently, the newly founded Tsukuba University launched a Faculty of Social Engineering and a Graduate Division of Policy Sciences, headed by an economist. Another national university, Saitama University, near Tokyo, is going to establish a Graduate Division of Policy Sciences.

However, according to a joint review of Japanese economic policy recently published by a group of economists (Masamura *et al.*, 1976, pp. 259–89), even in the field of formation of economic policy, when Japan was faced with a yen revaluation in the early 1970s, these policy-oriented economists failed to give effective advice, and the policy formation process was too irrational to follow such advice even if it had been presented. Masamura and his colleagues argue that a series of wrong economic policy choices were made in 1971 and 1972 with respect to the yen revaluation and control of the money supply, and that these wrong choices resulted in high-pitched inflation, which was accelerated by the oil crisis of 1973.

The example given by Masamura and his group indicates that a positive contribution by social scientists—in this case economists —depends not only on the social scientists, but also on the decision-makers, who in this case were Prime Minister Tanaka Kakuei, his Liberal Democratic Party, and business leaders with their strong inclination to encourage speculation and inflation, disregarding the advice of scholars or "government economists." Therefore, when we speak of the possible contribution of the social sciences to policy formation in a society, we have to take into consideration the political constellation of that particular society.

Social Changes in Japan—Recent Trends and Future Perspectives

Japan in the 1950s was a "middle advanced" society in terms of its economic development and in comparison with North America and West Europe. In 1955, 41 percent of Japan's labor force was engaged in primary industries, and per capita GNP was about U.S. $200, one-tenth that of the United States. In terms of social structure and values, changes introduced during the Occupation period (see Chapter 2) had not yet been completely consolidated. Although those changes were not just inventions of the Occupation but had certain indigenous necessities rooted in the development of Japanese society, they had the weakness of being introduced earlier and more abruptly than they would have emerged autonomously. Consequently, attack on the postwar reforms, on the one hand, and defense of them, on the other, became not only one of the vital political issues of the period between conservatives (before 1955, Liberal and Japan Democratic Parties; after 1955, Liberal Democratic Party) and socialists (before 1955, left-wing Socialist, right-wing Socialist, and Laborers and Farmers Parties; after 1955, Japan Socialist Party), but also a kind of cultural cleavage between those who preferred the "good old" social structure and values and those who found the postwar reforms rather congenial. Rural Japan was still the prototype of Japanese social structure and values in the 1950s, in spite of land reform and democratization of the family system. Dore (1959) and Fukutake (1964), in their studies of Japanese rural villages in this period, are describing not only the social system in rural villages but that of Japanese society as a whole.

Although Japan's economic growth, with its concomitant social changes, was already under way in the late 1950s (the annual economic growth rate in the late 1950s was already higher than 10 percent in nominal and 8 percent in substantial figures), the 1960s, which began under the Ikeda Cabinet's "low posture" and "income doubling plan" policies, saw a sustained high-growth economy and tremendous social changes unprecedented in Japan and incomparable with those of other industrial societies in terms of the speed of the changes.

The most conspicuous change of the 1960s was the shrinkage of the rural agricultural population. The percentage of the labor force engaging in primary industries dropped from 32.7 percent (14 million) in 1960 to 19.4 percent (10 million) in 1970, whereas the number of those engaging in secondary industries increased by 5 million and those in tertiary industries by nearly 8 million. Although, as Chapter 4 indicates, the rural world still often displays peculiar political behavior patterns, a majority of the electorate now works in secondary and tertiary industries.

The employees' sector of the work force became dominant in the 1960s, expanding from 23 million in 1960 to 33 million in 1970. What were the implications of the expansion of this group in terms of the dominant social structure in Japan and the value pattern of the Japanese people? Nakane (1967), whose work has been widely read both abroad and in Japan, argues that Japan's basic structure survived in the new supposedly "modern" businesses— and in all other Japanese organizations. Certainly, group solidarity and loyalty to the organization have been the basic characteristics of Japanese employees, and these characteristics were maintained and even reinforced during the 1960s, so that, in terms of social values, it can be said that shrinkage of the rural world and its value patterns was compensated for by the spread of Japanese organizational ethics to employed people.

However, in spite of the similarities between the new organizational ethics and the old rural norms, there is an important difference: in rural villages where people both lived and worked, people were under constant pressure to conform to the norms; whereas in organizations where people just work, they have the freedom to deviate outside the organization, in their free time. As a matter of fact, surveys showed increasingly diverse ways of life, ways of thinking, and values during the 1960s.

Another point which is often missed when the changes of the 1960s and their political significance are discussed is the persistence of the old urban middle class, which had always been a stronghold of traditional values and of political support for the conservatives. This group, consisting of small- and medium-sized manufacturers and wholesale or retail shopkeepers, increased in numbers and in wealth during this decade. According to the 1970 Census, the number of "self-proprietors in nonagricultural industries" grew from 4.6 million in 1960 to 6.0 million in 1970. With their three million family employees, this group remained a politically powerful group in terms of votes and of donations to the Liberal Democratic Party. (At the same time, the wealthier and better-educated part of this group has been the core of the enlightened and internationally minded local elite in most cities.)

The 1960s witnessed enormous rises in living standards, monetary incomes, and acquisition of consumer goods (see Chapter 3). People's expectations rose higher and higher, and both business and government were able to promise more and more. Consumption became a virtue, but the high personal savings rate of previous decades was also maintained throughout this decade of high and sustained economic growth.

In spite of a series of events which forced the Japanese economy to lower its economic growth rate—revaluation of the yen, the 1973 oil crisis, and various resource and environmental problems—certain changes seem to have continued from the 1960s or even to have accelerated. One is the change in the occupational structure: the 1975 Census showed that workers engaging in tertiary industries exceeded 50 percent of the total labor force. Another change which has been accelerated in the 1970s is the expansion of higher education and the corresponding increase in the number of university graduates in the labor force and the electorate. With the dominance of tertiary industry, the spread of higher education, and a per capita GNP of over $4,000 in 1975, and with an expected sustained growth of about 6 percent in years to come, Japan seems to qualify as a "postindustrial society," one in which knowledge and technology dominate.

However, if we look more carefully at occupational structure, we can easily see that Japan is still far from being such a "post-industrial society." In spite of the predominance of tertiary industries and the rapid increase in the number of university graduates, the census data show that the growth of professional and technical occupations is not keeping pace with the increasing number of people engaging in tertiary industries and the increasing number of university graduates. Furthermore, Japanese organizational practices of lifelong employment and advancement by seniority discourage professionalization because, with their emphasis on company loyalty, they hinder professional mobility and the formation of professional ethics.

The tendency toward diversification of value patterns has been enhanced in the early 1970s. In the late 1960s, environmentalist values began emerging, and they became more influential after people became disillusioned with the rampant inflation and frenzied land speculation which began under the Tanaka government and was fueled by the oil crisis. Demand for popular participation in decision making, especially at the local level, also emerged in the late 1960s and increased in the 1970s. In local elections, every candidate can now be heard encouraging citizens' participation. Protest actions directed against decisions of the national government have spread even to peripheral parts of the polity.

But here, too, we cannot speak of the predominance of "post-industrial values" yet, nor can we anticipate an indefinite expansion of their influence in the future. First of all, wages and prices of commodities are still people's major concerns—understandably, given the continued rise in prices and the scarcity and cost of land and housing in Japanese cities. Second, some features of Japanese traditional values are similar to postindustrial values, which not only makes measurement of values in Japan complicated but also makes future prediction difficult. For example, to avoid conflict and to lay emphasis on harmony or conformity are traditional Japanese values. In Ronald Inglehart's new post-industrial values survey, one of the postindustrial values in the questionnaire is phrased as "move toward a friendlier, less impersonal society." When I used one of Inglehart's questions in Japan, this indicator phrased in this way attracted the second largest share of responses (next to "stability of economy"). Some will be delighted to hear this result and will argue that Japanese traditional values deserve to be restored even in a postindustrial age. But I believe that not all Japanese traditional values should be or can be restored. For instance, emperor worship and unconditional obedience to the superior cannot be restored any more. So the question is what part of Japanese traditional values can be revived functionally, and what would a combined constellation of revived old values and postwar values look like? This subject needs further exploration.

Democracy and Postwar Politics

Beginning with disclosures before a committee in the U.S. Senate in February 1976, the Lockheed bribery scandal shattered Japanese political circles and threw the Liberal Democratic Party—Japan's party in power for more than twenty years—into serious disarray. I would argue that the scandal was a crisis for the LDP's rule, not for Japanese democracy itself. Nevertheless, since the LDP has been the ruling party of Japan for more than two decades and there is no single powerful opposition party to replace it, there is some truth in the idea that the crisis of the LDP is the crisis of Japanese politics.

Japan faced that kind of crisis in the late 1950s, just after the end of the Occupation, and the early 1960s (see Chapter 5). Fortunately, Japanese democracy, which was "implanted" during the U.S. Occupation (though not without indigenous support), survived the attacks of the Japanese conservatives. The Japan Socialist Party performed the central role in the defense of postwar democracy.

The 1960s brought consolidation of postwar democracy on the one hand, and on the other prepared the way to such corruption as that revealed by the Lockheed bribery scandal. The LDP,

under the leadership of prime ministers Ikeda Hayato and Satō
Eisaku, ceased to attempt seriously to change the 1947 Constitution. Institutions such as the nonauthoritarian family system, labor
unions, and local autonomy, which were introduced in the postwar period, had established themselves completely not only in
terms of support by the general public but also in terms of acceptance by the rather conservative business circles, which, with
high economic growth and its concomitant social changes, found
those institutions to be congruent with their business activities.

On the other hand, the LDP's single-party rule throughout this
period built up a peculiar system of rule which, in the 1970s, is
neither workable nor maintainable. Four characteristics of that
system can be outlined. One: the top leaders of the LDP, high
bureaucrats, and business leaders had built up close mutual networks, and this triumvirate, in spite of occasional minor disagree-
ments, took fairly coordinated action in deciding vital policies in
the 1960s. Business circles provided the bulk of the LDP's political
funds through Keidanren (Federation of Economic Organizations) via the Kokuminkyōkai (National Association). High-
ranking bureaucrats cooperated with the LDP leaders, and, in
exchange for their services during their active duty, they were
given high positions in big business or in semigovernmental organizations, or they could run for the Diet, heavily sponsored by
the LDP leaders, after their usually rather early retirement at 50
to 55 years of age.

Two: the LDP built up a huge vote-getting mechanism at the
local level, coping with the shrinkage of the rural world which was
once a natural basis for conservative rule. Every LDP politician—
whether incumbent or possible candidate—has built up his or her
own *kōenkai* (personal sponsoring association) in his or her constitu-
ency. In order to build and maintain powerful *kōenkai*, politicians
need money and the ability to channel government benefits to
their particular constituencies. Through this "organizational clientelism" (see Chapter 3), the LDP and its politicians guarded
the diverse occupational and local interests of their constituents.
Due to the rapid increase in governmental revenue and spending
during the high-growth period of the 1960s, the LDP and its
politicians could increase the benefit to their constituencies. In
this respect, the LDP's rule was beneficial not solely to big busi-

ness, but also to local and other diversified interests. However, massive spending on public construction became the basis for the corruption of the LDP and its politicians. Because their *kōenkai* were not able to collect membership dues and personal donations on a mass basis, almost all of the LDP politicians chose the easy way of getting necessary political funds, either from their faction leaders within the LDP or from private enterprises—sometimes from big companies at the national level and sometimes from medium- and small-sized local companies, among which the construction companies were the most generous donors. Faction leaders in the LDP had to gather huge funds in order to take care of the monetary needs of their faction members and so to maintain the strength of their factions within the LDP.

Three: when the LDP was formed in 1955, the original pattern was set by those old politicians whose party experiences were in the prewar parties, when a political party was simply a collection of politicians. They had no idea of mass party organization or of membership dues as the basis of party finance. Political funds were to be raised by the boss, and it was natural for politicians to gather around powerful and humane bosses within the party. This kind of political culture was maintained and even reinforced during the 1960s, in spite of sporadic calls for and halfhearted formal attempts at party reform which brought no results at all. The LDP's vote-getting system had worked well enough to assure it a majority of the seats in the Diet.

Four: the LDP, though in the majority, made it a rule to tolerate extremely prolonged Diet sessions—often extending to 200 days in a year—and to negotiate with the opposition parties in procedural matters. On the surface, this made the LDP the most tolerant majority party in the world. However, in reality, this practice weakened the functions of the Diet, because almost all important policies were determined within the LDP, and only the formal procedures were discussed prolongedly with the opposition parties, with little time and emphasis being given to substantial deliberation.

In spite of all these well-established, effective, and neither illegal nor totally immoral mechanisms of LDP rule consolidated in the 1960s, the gradual decline of the party's share of the votes in national elections and the defeat of LDP candidates in gubernatorial elections in metropolitan areas were characteristic of the late 1960s (see Chapter 3).

Following Satō Eisaku's retirement in 1972 after seven years and eight months' rule as prime minister, Tanaka Kakuei became president of the LDP and prime minister of Japan in July 1972. Tanaka was a skilled manipulator of "organizational clientelism" during the 1960s and showed outstanding ability to raise funds. Seeing the gradual decline in the LDP's share of the votes, he felt a mission to reverse that situation, based on his belief that to raise and spend any amount of money in any way was perfectly legitimate. As the president of the LDP, in the general election of December 1972, and especially in the House of Councillors election in July 1974, he and his aides spent unprecedentedly huge sums of money, both on behalf of the LDP and on behalf of his own faction. But Tanaka's strategy failed. In the House of Councillors election, the LDP retained only a slim majority, and its share of the vote fell to less than 40 percent in prefectural districts. Tanaka's "money election" was severely criticized by the mass media, and Miki Takeo and Fukuda Takeo, both vice-prime ministers in Tanaka's cabinet, resigned in protest against Tanaka's "money politics."

As a journalist put it, Tanaka was "a hero who came belatedly": on the one hand, he pursued and consummated the typical LDP behavior pattern in the high economic growth period of the 1960s, and in that sense, he was a hero. On the other hand, the tide had begun to change, making the behavior pattern, which worked so well in the 1950s and 1960s, less workable in the 1970s. In that sense, he came belatedly.

How is the tide changing in the 1970s? For one thing, even business circles have found Tanaka's way of spending money excessive, especially under conditions of decelerated economic growth. Another more serious change is the increase in the number of independent voters, whose votes cannot be solicited by the political and campaigning styles of either the LDP or any other party. I believe that this phenomenon is related to the rising educational level and the activities of the Japanese mass media, in spite of their definite shortcomings (see Chapter 1).

The Lockheed bribery scandal and the arrest and prosecution of Tanaka and other high-ranking politicians will trigger further changes. It seems to be only a matter of time before the LDP loses its absolute majority of seats in the Diet, although it will still be Japan's largest party. Thus Japanese democracy is now entering a period of reshuffling hitherto established political styles and creating new ones. It remains to be seen what those new political styles will be. But what is certain is that they will be, within the scope of democracy, better in the ethical sense and no less workable than the styles of the 1960s which culminated in the Lockheed bribery scandal.

Japan, Asia, and the World

Any society in the "modern" world cannot exist in complete isolation from other societies. However, the degree of interdependence differs from society to society and, within a society, from period to period. Japanese society and the Japanese nation, awakened from over two hundred years' dormancy by the West, successfully responded to the West's challenge to modernize economically and politically, but also displayed Western aggressive behavior toward its neighbors, Korea and China. Chapter 7 discusses and tries to draw more general insights into the dominance problem between neighboring societies. Chapter 8 is a tentative attempt to extend the insights obtained from Japan's nation-building experience to Southeast Asia.

After its defeat in World War II, Japan sometimes seemed, to use an extreme expression, to be going back to the isolation of the Edo period, in its inward-looking stance under the U.S. nuclear umbrella. However, during the 1960s, Japan's economic weight in the world rapidly increased, although its military weight did not.

However, the assumption of a more positive role in the world corresponding to this increased economic weight has tended to lag behind (see Chapter 9). The assumption of such an active role is not simple, in part because, since Japan is in East Asia and has historically had a close relationship with China, the presence of China has sometimes constrained both Japanese decision-makers and the Japanese public. The survey data in Chapter 9 illustrate Japan's somewhat divided identity as an East Asian nation and also as an industrially advanced society.

Part I

The Nature of Japanese Democracy

Chapter I
Japan's Governability as a Democracy

There is no absolute governability or ungovernability. Governability is always a function of tasks, both imposed from outside and generated from the inside, and of capabilities. In discussing the governability of democracy in Japan, the place to start is with the reforms after World War II and the 1947 Constitution, which is the key political institution of postwar Japanese democracy. The Japanese Constitution of 1947 was prepared under the U.S. Occupation. The draft was written by the staff of SCAP (Supreme Commander for the Allied Powers) and General Douglas MacArthur, and handed to the Japanese government with strong pressure in early 1946.

However, in spite of its apparent imposition or implantation by the Allied—actually American—Occupation forces, and in spite of a tenacious movement by rightists both outside and inside the Liberal Democratic Party to abolish this "given Constitution" and to make an "autonomous" constitution, the 1947 Constitution has been in operation for thirty years and is likely to remain intact for the foreseeable future, including its unique Article 9 which forbids Japan to wage war as a nation and to maintain armed forces. It is a miracle of modern history and is a key to understanding and predicting Japanese society and politics.

The miracle occurred for three good reasons. In the first place, the draft Constitution prepared by SCAP was not written in a void. It had many ideas in common with a draft constitution prepared by Japanese liberals at that time. Besides the Constitution itself, many postwar reforms carried out under the Occupation were congruent with (or some steps in advance of) the proposals made by the liberals and even by enlightened bureaucrats at that time or even in prewar days. Thus, many reforms during the Occupation helped to release and encourage "reform potentials" which had already accumulated in Japan during World War II.

Second, a positive role was played by the opposition—especially the Japan Socialist Party in the 1952–55 period, just after the end of the Occupation. The conservatives, at that time consisting of the Liberal Party and the Japan Democratic Party, wanted to revise the "excessive" reforms made under the Occupation and campaigned for rewriting the whole Constitution. The key parts of the Constitution which the conservatives wanted to rewrite were those treating the status of the Emperor, Article 9, and those concerning the family system. Extreme conservatives wanted more general deliberalization of the rights of labor unions, freedom of speech and association, and so on. If their attempts had been successful, what would the consequences have been for Japanese society and politics? Since this is a matter of sheer conjecture, it is open to various arguments. My argument, however, is this: The consequence would have been less stability in Japanese politics and the accumulation of more frustration and alienation among the better-educated and younger people in Japanese society. A Japan with established armed forces but with more domestic political confrontation, and possibly with repeated attempts at constitutional revision in both radical and reactionary directions, might have resulted. As it was, the Socialists, who at that time were divided between a right wing and a left wing but who all agreed to preserve the 1947 Constitution, succeeded in winning one-third of the seats in both Houses of the Diet in elections in the early 1950s and blocked the conservatives' attempt to revise the Constitution, which required the approval of two-thirds of the Diet. The legacy of the constitutional dispute in this period still remains in the habitual way of thinking of the 1947 Constitution as one package, no part of which can be revised without rewriting the whole.

Third, during the period of economic growth in the late 1950s and throughout the 1960s, and its concomitant social changes, the 1947 Constitution and most of the postwar reforms became quite compatible with the operation of the Japanese economy and society. The objections raised by the conservatives, especially in the late 1950s by the ultra-rightists among them, to the 1947 Constitution became obsolete in the 1960s. For example, the 1947

Constitution and the reform of the family code assured the independence of family members. Younger people, who were supposed to be under the control of the family head before the reforms, were given legal freedom from the family by the postwar reforms; but they also received economic freedom because of the demand for labor and the high wages in the 1960s. From the viewpoint of industry, voluntary mobility of younger people irrespective of the assent of the family head was welcome. Labor unions, which were recognized and protected by the 1947 Constitution, with their peculiarly Japanese form of "enterprise unions," were found to be no obstacle to technological innovation and to contribute to the commitment of the workers to the company.

Thus, the mainstream of the Liberal Democratic Party and the mainstream of Japanese economic circles have no serious intention of revising the 1947 Constitution now or in the near future, in spite of some occasional rhetoric to that effect in the LDP platform. According to opinion polls, the majority of the public also supports the 1947 Constitution. The Socialist and the Kōmei Parties are firmly committed to it. The Japan Communist Party has also declared its commitment to defend the present Constitution, at least in the near future, although at the same time it does not hide its view that at some remote future time the Constitution should be rewritten in a more "socialistic" style.

Thus, in comparison with the German Weimar Republic of 1919–33, Japanese postwar democracy has a firm basis. The suspicion is sometimes voiced that the Japanese people have accepted the postwar democratic system primarily because of Japan's economic prosperity in the postwar period. However, even if this is so, the prewar system offers no competing attraction, especially to the younger generation. There is little possibility of a powerful revival of prewar Japanese militarism or political authoritarianism in the future. Rather, the problem is how, within the bounds of the 1947 Constitution, Japan can handle the status of the Self-Defense Forces, which on the one hand have been regarded by the Socialist and the Communist Parties as unconstitutional, and on the other hand have accumulated *de facto* legitimacy during twenty years of development under the LDP government.

The Capability of the Liberal Democratic Party

The Japanese conservatives, particularly the Liberal Democratic Party since its formation in 1955, have ruled Japan throughout the postwar period, except for the short and unsuccessful coalition of the Socialist and Democratic Parties in 1947–48. The capability of the LDP is open to dispute. LDP members and supporters can say that Japan's economic growth and its peaceful existence with other nations are proof of the LDP's high capability. The award of the 1974 Nobel Peace Prize to former Prime Minister Satō Eisaku seems to support such an argument. But the opposition parties have naturally been critical of the LDP's capability and of the award of the Nobel Prize to Satō. Apart from such partisan disputes, two observations can be made. First, the LDP's rule has had both merits and demerits—in other words, it has been both functional and dysfunctional. Second, the social and cultural traits which have hitherto supported the LDP have been declining in importance. Thus, Japanese society seems to be less congruent with the LDP than before.

As for the LDP's merits, I can cite three points. First, the close coordination between the LDP, the higher elite corps of the bureaucracy, and the economic elite (which have collectively been called "Japan Incorporated" since *Time* magazine's story of May 10, 1971, invented the term) certainly contributed to Japan's economic growth in the 1960s. Certainly the LDP's capability for policy formation has been high in the sense that it has been aided by infusions of ex-high-level bureaucrats, who became either LDP parliamentary members or top executives of public and private corporations after their relatively early retirements. Ex-high-level bureaucrats, as LDP politicians, contribute the knowledge and experience accumulated during their bureaucratic careers to the formation of policies by the party. They also maintain communication with their ex-colleagues in public and private corporations and with their successors on active duty in the bureaucracy.

Second, the LDP has built up skillful vote-getting machines in its *kōenkai*, associations supporting individual politicians, through which various demands—personal, regional, and occupational—of the populace have been absorbed and satisfied. LDP politicians are very responsive to their *kōenkai*, especially to the key persons

in them, who are often influential in local agricultural associations
or small- and medium-sized trade associations. Therefore, in spite
of its close coordination with big businesses and its financial de-
pendence on them, the LDP has not ignored the interests of local
leaders in farming, fishing, small- and medium-sized commerce,
and manufacturing. The LDP at the grassroots level has been
loosely structured and has consisted of federations of hundreds of
small parties. Therefore, it has been able to absorb a variety of
interests and demands. As is well known, however, mainly because
of the need for money, LDP politicians are "aggregated" into
several factions, and ultimately the formation of LDP policy is
made in close contact with the bureaucracy and big businesses.
Thus, in a sense, we see a pattern of wide interest articulation
through individual LDP members and their *kōenkai*, interest aggregation through factions, and eventual agreement by the triumvirate of big business, bureaucracy, and the LDP.

Third, although the LDP has been self-identified as a conservative party and many members of it have expressed nostalgia for
a number of aspects of the prewar system from time to time, and
although a close tie with the United States has been the LDP's
official line on foreign policy, still LDP Diet members have enjoyed a wide range of freedom to express divergent policy views
and even behavior concerning both domestic and foreign policies.
In the sphere of foreign policy, members of the Asian and African
Problem Study Group visited the People's Republic of China a
number of times before Tanaka's official visit to China in 1972,
and also have been in contact with the Democratic People's Republic of Korea. However, the LDP still has strong Taiwan supporters and also a South Korean lobby, composed of those who
keep close ties with the Republic of Korea. In the sphere of domestic policy, a fairly wide divergence of opinion exists among
LDP politicians. This ideological looseness and vagueness of the
LDP is due to the independence of LDP politicians in vote-getting
and to the nonideological formation of factions within the LDP;
these characteristics have, in their turn, contributed to neutraliz-
ing the opposition charge that the LDP is a reactionary party.
These characteristics have, moreover, given the LDP wider channels of contact and assets to be utilized in policy making.

All of these "merits," on the other hand, also involve dysfunctions. Close contact and skillful coordination in the LDP-business-bureaucracy triumvirate has meant the disproportional predominance of business and bureaucratic interests in policy formation. Powers to countervail and check that triumvirate have been disproportionately weak. As for the *kōenkai*, which have made the LDP capable of absorbing various interests and demands, since they are not distributed equally in terms of region, occupation, and generation, unavoidably some interests are systematically respected and others are ignored. Continuation of LDP rule for over twenty years has generated a sense of alienation from power and a feeling of ill-treatment in certain sectors of society. To supporters of the opposition parties, not only LDP rule but also the whole period of Japanese history under LDP rule is subject to criticism. It has been *their* rule, and *their* period, not *ours*, from this perspective. The looseness of ideological control within the LDP has given rise to the widely held fear of unpredictability in LDP behavior. Some policies are formed on the basis of factional fights or compromise within the LDP, and many others are made upon consultation with, or according to the advice of, bureaucratic and business circles. The LDP can suddenly propose ultraconservative, even rightist, policies. Partly because of this unpredictability, a lack of trust between governing party and opposition parties has been conspicuous.

An ethical weakness of the LDP is its way of procuring and spending political funds. All LDP politicians have to constantly procure and spend money in order to maintain their own *kōenkai*. The minimum necessary expenditure of LDP Diet members is said to be three million yen (10,000 U.S. dollars) per month in a nonelection period. They raise part of this money themselves, and part comes from their faction leaders. The major part of these political funds is given by business corporations. Are huge sums of political donations by business corporations really pure and voluntary contributions, or is this implicit bribery? And is it fair for the LDP and LDP factions combined to spend five times more than the total spent by all four opposition parties together, according to an official report released by the government?[1]

[1]According to a report on political funds compiled by the Home Affairs Ministry for the first half of 1974, out of a registered total of ¥51.6 billion ($170 million), the LDP and its factions together got ¥40 billion (*Yomiuri shimbun*, December 25, 1974). Moreover, it is widely believed that, if "hidden money" is taken into account, the

The LDP's share of the votes in national elections has been gradually declining. In the general election for the House of Representatives held in December 1976, the LDP's share of the votes dropped to 41.8 percent, 5 percent lower than that in the previous election of 1972. Partly due to the overrepresentation of rural districts in the distribution of the seats and partly due to the joining of nonpartisan conservative winners to the LDP after the election, the LDP maintained a slim majority in the House (260 seats out of total 511 seats, as of January 1977). However, in the House of Councillors, the LDP's majority is slimmer (127 seats out of 252, as of January 1977), and the LDP may lose its majority in the coming election of July 1977.

Quality of the Japanese Bureaucracy

In any understanding of governability as a synthetic capability relating the governing and the governed, the quality of bureaucracy, as the governing framework, as an intermediary between the governing and the governed, or as an autonomous third force, has special significance. In this respect, the Japanese bureaucracy seems to deserve some attention. Historically, the Japanese bureaucracy was formed after the Prussian model, with its formalistic legalism and alleged neutralism—which does not, however, prevent high-level bureaucrats from committing themselves to partisan stands of the governing party, as representing the interest of the state. Many high-level bureaucrats, after retirement, have joined the LDP and become key figures in the governing party. The bureaucrats on duty are, however, fairly autonomous under the control of administrative vice-ministers, and the elite bureaucratic corps has a high degree of *esprit de corps* similar to that of the British Civil Service.[2] During the recent period of economic growth, mainly in the Ministries of Finance and of International Trade and Industry and in the Economic Planning Agency, tech-

LDP is spending more. For instance, it was pointed out that the actual sum of money the LDP and its factions spent in 1972 was nearly ¥100 billion, although the official record for that year was ¥26 billion (*Bungei shunju*, September 1974).

[2] In a survey of bureau and section chiefs in the national bureaucracy, 37 percent answered that they are independent when asked about their party preference. In the Ministry of International Trade and Industry (MITI), a majority chose the independent position (Nikkei Business Henshūbu, 1974, pp. 182–83).

nocrats, primarily economic specialists, have been gaining power; in this predominance of technocrats, Japanese bureaucracy can be compared with the French bureaucracy.

Thus, the capability of the Japanese bureaucracy can be evaluated as rather high. The members of the elite bureaucratic corps, consisting of those who passed the higher civil service examination —whose number is still limited to 400 or so annually in this age of expansion of higher education with 1.5 million university students—are really elite in terms both of their initial caliber and of the opportunities for training and accumulation of administrative experience given to them during their careers. This elite bureaucratic corps of about ten thousand is still prepared to work twenty-four hours a day and seven days a week if necessary, because of its privileged position and the prevailing ethos of diligence and self-sacrifice in the elite corps.

There are, however, dysfunctions and vulnerabilities in the Japanese bureaucracy. The top level of the bureaucratic elite corps and alumni from this group have been too fused with the LDP. Furthermore, with the expansion of higher education, a system designed to recruit only four hundred or so per year to the elite bureaucratic corps cannot maintain itself forever. Many university graduates are taking examinations for middle civil service positions which have been intended for high school or junior college graduates. In such a situation it will become difficult to give special favors to those who passed higher civil service examinations and to discriminate against other members of the bureaucracy who are now also university graduates. In not so remote a future the notion and practice of the elite bureaucratic corps will be forced to give way to more egalitarian, less privileged forms.

In addition, it has been an established practice for Japanese ministries to recruit their own personnel, both elite and nonelite. The aim has been to build up the ministry's own bureaucracy of specialists on matters over which that ministry presides and to build up strong solidarity in the elite bureaucratic corps within a particular ministry. This practice has brought with it the pattern of ministerial bureaucrats acting to promote the interests of their clients and ardently promoting interests and demands within their jurisdictions even in dispute with the governing party, thus serving as guardians of interests which might be neglected by the governing party. But the cost paid for this is bureaucratic section-alism, and there is no bureau to take care of overall policy. To be sure, there are the Prime Minister's Office and the Cabinet Secretariat, which are supposed to perform this function, but these officials come from various ministries, serve for a couple of years, and go back to their home ministries; therefore, they are likely to remain committed to the particular interests of their home ministries.

The Economy

As is well known, Japanese economic growth during the two decades before the oil crisis of October 1973 was amazing, con-tinuously showing an annual increase of over 10 percent. GNP and per capita income doubled every five years. Even considering the rises in commodity prices, real wages still nearly doubled between 1960 and 1972. Japan's GNP is larger than that of any West European country, and its per capita income or wage is roughly equal to, or even slightly higher than, those in Britain or France, depending on the statistics used. With this growth of GNP and in-crease of per capita income and wages, government revenue and spending have expanded enormously. From 1965 to 1973, for instance, the government budget grew from 3,658 billion yen to 14,284 billion yen—that is, over three times.[3] In other words, so far, with the growth of the Japanese economy, the government has acquired tremendous amounts of goods and services which it can dispose of, and this has made it possible for the Japanese govern-ment to distribute goods and services in response to the increased demands of the populace. Under these circumstances, government has been able to avoid serious priority problems.

However, since the revaluation of the yen, the oil crisis, and the subsequent jump in oil prices, the picture has been changing rapidly. The growth rate for fiscal year 1973 (April 1973 to 1974) dropped sharply to 5.4 percent, and that for fiscal 1974 was eventually found to be negative (−1.8 percent). According to the

[3]These figures include the general account but do not include special accounts and governmental investment; they include the starting budget but do not include any ad-ditions; and they are nominal values.

Ministry of International Trade and Industry (MITI), the expected growth rate for 1975 is 2 percent. Although somewhat slowed, the rise of consumer prices as of March 1975 in comparison with the previous year was still 13 percent. In this economic situation, the national government could still increase its budget to 17,180 billion yen in the 1974 fiscal year and 21,280 billion yen in fiscal 1975, without creating serious deficits and increasing the rate of inflation, but local governments now face serious deficits in their budgets. It is expected that the national government too will face a tighter financial situation and priority problems in budget making for the fiscal year beginning in April 1976.

The government has defined the period from 1974 to 1976 as an adjustment period from rapid economic growth to stable economic growth or a "less accelerated" economy, as it is called. After 1976, MITI is expecting an annual economic growth rate of about 7 percent. If so, this moderate growth can give some leeway for priority problems, but that leeway will be far more restricted than in years of more than 10 percent growth.

Mass Media

Development of mass media in Japan is quite conspicuous. The total number of copies of newspapers issued daily is 56 million, which is second only to that in the United States (63 million copies). The estimated number of television sets currently in use is 48 million, and there are five nationwide television networks—one is the publicly operated NHK (Japan Broadcasting Corporation) and the other four are privately owned (NTV, TBS, Fuji, and NET). Besides the press and TV, the plethora of magazines is a characteristic of the Japanese mass media scene. In particular, the variety of weekly magazines with huge circulations (about fifty different weekly magazines are selling eight million copies per month) is striking (Shikauchi, 1974).

Under the postwar democracy, there has been no governmental censorship except during the Occupation period, and all the major newspapers and TV networks have been avowed guardians of democracy. Their quality is not bad, especially the five major newspapers with nationwide circulation (*Asahi, Mainichi, Yomiuri, San-kei,* and *Nihon keizai*), which are proud of being quality news-papers with circulations of several million each.

Thus we can say that the Japanese mass media as a whole are a positive factor in the maintenance and operation of Japanese democracy. However, the Japanese mass media have several characteristics peculiar to Japan which function as a kind of con-straint, within which Japanese democracy has to operate and which might make Japanese democracy vulnerable under changed conditions.

First, as has often been pointed out, Japanese newspapers are highly standardized, in the sense that they tend to refrain from presenting partisan opinion and allocate their space in a quite similar way to coverage of everything from on-the-street human interest stories to highbrow academic articles.

A second established characteristic of Japanese newspapers is what is called their "opposition spirit," which means they are criti-cal of the government, but within the limits of nonpartisanship. The result is that nonpartisan intellectual radicalism is treated rather favorably in the newspapers and a tone of moral sensa-tionalism colors the reports and articles in newspapers.

In the case of broadcasting, NHK clings more strictly to the principle of nonpartisanship and to a less critical spirit than the newspapers. Other TV networks are more and more tied to partic-ular major newspapers and show similar characteristics to these newspapers in their reporting. However, sensationalism is more obvious in several weekly magazines, such as *Shūkan posuto, Shūkan gendai* and (although in a rather conservative tone) *Shūkan shinchō*, each of which sells over 500,000 copies every week.

These characteristics of the Japanese mass media can have both positive and negative implications for Japanese democracy. The newspapers' and NHK's nonpartisanship is useful in prevent-ing manipulation by the powerful mass media. Sensationalism has helped to arouse the attention of the public to issues as they arise. Nonpartisanship can also mean the loss of the function of stimu-lating political discussion, however, and the critical spirit and moral sensationalism can encourage political distrust of govern-ment.

Education

Expansion of higher education in Japan has been amazing during the past decade. The percentage of those enrolling in universities and colleges among the eligible age group has doubled during the decade and reached 30 percent in 1974. Furthermore, it is expected that this trend will continue and that enrollment will reach 40 percent by 1980. From an educational standpoint, the Japanese university system has a number of problems (see OECD, 1970), but only the political relevance of this expansion of higher education will be considered here.

So far, university expansion has had relatively little direct impact on politics. Of course, there has been sporadic campus unrest, emergence of a variety of radical groups recruited from university students, and participation of a number of students in antipollution movements. Also, the Japan Communist Party has maintained its influence on student movements through its Democratic Youth League, and the League's members are quite active in JCP's election campaigns. However, a majority of the 1.5 million Japanese university students and the millions of recent graduates have been relatively calm politically. One of the reasons for this calm has been the favorable situation in the job market for the rapidly increasing numbers of university graduates. The decade has witnessed an enormous expansion of tertiary industries and of professional, technical, and clerical jobs, which have absorbed several million university graduates. The shortage of young blue-collar workers resulted in the improvement of the wages not only of young blue-collar workers but also of young white-collar workers. In spite of an ongoing change of values in the younger generation, organizational constraints regulating the new recruits in business or bureaucracy have persisted and have been successful in making them adapt to organizational norms. Moreover, so far the expansion of higher education has coincided with the expansion of local governmental activities and personnel. The percentage of university graduates among newly recruited civil servants on the local government level has increased rapidly, and this has certainly contributed to upgrading the quality of the local civil service.

The crucial question, however, is whether the Japanese economy can continue to offer suitable jobs to university graduates who constitute over 30 percent or even 40 percent of the corresponding age group. Another important question is the cost and quality of higher education. The government has been increasing the appropriation of public funds to assist private universities. In the expected tight budgetary situation, whether government can and should expand such assistance is questionable.

Labor Unions

In postwar Japanese democracy, labor unions have established their position firmly. Japanese labor unions with their unique form of "enterprise union"—meaning that unions have been organized primarily within each company, embracing all employees in that company—have had no essential objection to the introduction of technological innovations so long as the company has guaranteed favorable treatment and offered retraining to those who were transferred to new jobs in the company, unlike British unions based on a particular job or craft. In spite of their basic enterprise-union form, Japanese labor unions have succeeded in building up federations of unions within the same kinds of industries, and eventually even national federations of labor unions. (Sōhyō and Dōmei are two big national federations of labor unions which have been exercising fairly strong influence through their jointly scheduled plan of wage-raise demands (the so-called "spring offensive") and electoral campaigning in support of the opposition parties. Sōhyō supports the Socialists and Dōmei supports the Democratic Socialists.)

Present-day democracy cannot exist without the recognition of and support from labor unions. In Japan's case, even the LDP government, which has had no labor union to support it, cannot ignore labor unions and has placed representatives of Sōhyō and Dōmei on a number of deliberation councils on labor administration and also on labor relations committees. But essentially, the LDP has been on the side of business and more concerned with the interests of its supporters—farmers and small- and medium-size manufacturers. One might argue that it has been rather a good balance since organized labor has had a powerful say even if it has not been respected by the LDP. The opposite argument is that organized labor should have been respected more in order to counterbalance the influence of big business on LDP governments, and that organized labor has been representing the interests of not only its members but also all those who have been unfavorably treated under LDP governments. The third view, which has been emerging recently, does not trust either LDP governments or labor unions. It insists that since labor unions represent the interests of only a fraction of the total population (only about 30 percent of the employed are organized into labor unions) and since the two national federations represent an even smaller fraction (Sōhyō, with its 4.5 million membership, organizes 12 percent; Dōmei, with its 2.2 million membership, 6 percent of the total employed), the interests of ordinary citizens should be respected more; that is, emerging consumers' movements and various citizens' movements should be respected more than, or at least alongside, organized labor in order to increase the responsiveness of Japanese democracy.

External Conditions

Although there seems to be no impending external threat of military aggression to Japan, there exist uncertainties of a military nature which, if they should be actualized, would impose enormous strains on Japanese leaders. One is the instability of the Korean situation and a possible escalating confrontation between the Republic of Korea and the Democratic People's Republic of Korea. Another is the possibility of Sino-Soviet military confrontation. In both cases, if the conflicts should escalate enough, they would cause worldwide repercussions, and the United States, at least, would inevitably be involved in them. If, however, the escalation should remain below certain limits and could be regarded as a local problem, it is possible that strong pressures to force Japanese decision-makers to make difficult policy decisions would be applied from both sides of the conflict. The Korean problem also has a special significance for the internal governability of Japan, because of its large number of Korean residents.

Apart from such critical and, hopefully, improbable cases, there are two external factors which create problems for Japan and for the Japanese leadership. One is the well-known international dependency and vulnerability of the Japanese economy in terms of natural resources not only for industry but also for feeding the Japanese people. According to often-cited figures, Japan's ratio of dependency on overseas resources is: almost 100 percent in oil; 85 percent in total energy supply; 100 percent in bauxite; and 95 percent in iron ore (1970 level). Of Japan's total food supply, 23 percent comes from abroad; among vital foodstuffs, 92 percent of the wheat and 96 percent of the soybeans consumed in Japan in 1971 came from abroad. In comparison with the equivalent figures for the United States, these figures are impressive enough to show Japan's international dependency in the acquisition of resources.

Japan's dependency is, however, on the same level as that of many West European societies. What distinguishes Japan from West European societies is the second external factor: Japan stands alone in its region with no equal partner for joint action which would share common interests due to a similar stage of industrial development, combined with the same degree of commitment to principles of political democracy. Of course, in spite of the European Community, West European countries are far from achieving complete accord and being able to take united action to cope with their difficulties. And West European countries and the European Community as a whole always have to take into consideration the moves of other regions—those of the Soviet bloc, the Arab countries, and all other Third World countries. Japan is the most economically advanced country in Asia, on the one hand, but because of the historical relationship between Japan and the countries of Asia, the Japanese are torn between a feeling of belonging to Asia and a feeling of isolation from Asia, with "Western" orientation. On the other hand, the Asian countries are also ambivalent toward Japan. The Japanese, including those in other Asian countries, are expected to perform a positive role because they are Asians; at the same time they are often severely criticized for behavior which would be permitted in Europeans or Americans. This delicate position of Japan in the region can be made to serve as an asset linking the other Asian countries with the Western societies with advanced economies. On the other hand, it could become a liability which could confuse Japan's policy choices and aggravate the tensions between the developing countries and the economically advanced countries.

The 1947 Constitution as a Package: The Key Political Belief

Since values determine the way people think and act, it is important to see how changing values, which are most conspicuously observable in the younger generation and are expected to continue changing in years to come, will affect the governability of Japanese democracy. All the survey data collected in recent years reinforce the point that there is no sign of weakening in the support for the 1947 Constitution. On the contrary, younger and better-educated people tend to support more strongly the 1947 Constitution as a whole, including its Article 9 forbidding Japan to wage war and to have armed forces for that purpose. Therefore, the 1947 Constitution has become a given.

It is sometimes argued that the Japanese "warlike" national character will not change so easily; therefore, if the international situation changes slightly, the Japanese will easily change their minds and discard the 1947 Constitution, especially its Article 9. But this kind of argument, which is often found among overseas Chinese scholars, is highly improbable. Another argument stresses that if some grave change should occur in international relations —in other words, if some real threat of aggression to Japan by some foreign powers should occur—the Japanese "mood" would change rapidly to support rearmament and consequently a revision of the 1947 Constitution. The possibility certainly exists, but this argument seems to be based on unlikely assumptions.

Emergence of Participation and Protest Movements

An ongoing change is occurring, which is not incompatible with the beliefs in the 1947 Constitution but is not identical with it, and which will exercise a far-reaching influence on the future of Japanese democracy. It is a change from submissiveness to authority to active protest and demands for participation—that is, from "subject" political culture to "participatory" political culture. The questionnaire responses shown in Table 1.1 illustrate this change.

Table 1.1:   Views on a politician's duty. Responses to the question: "In order to improve the Japanese nation, do you agree or disagree with the statement that, if a competent politician is available, it is better to leave things to him rather than discuss them among ordinary citizens?" (in percentages)

	Agree	Case by case	Disagree	Others, D. K., N. A.	
1953	43	9	38	10	(N = 2,254)
1958	35	10	44	11	(N = 2,369)
1963	29	12	47	12	(N = 2,698)
1968	30	10	51	9	(N = 3,033)
1973	23	15	51	11	(N = 3,055)

Source: Institute of Mathematical Statistics (1974).

Two comments are specially warranted on Table 1.1. When the first survey was conducted in 1953, a majority of Japanese over twenty years old were prepared to leave things to competent politicians, if such were available. In other words, at that time, the majority of the masses were prepared to obey a competent politician; therefore, the governability problem was simply whether such competent politicians were available or not. During the period of economic growth, people became more self-assertive and began to dislike leaving things even to competent politicians. So, the governability problem becomes not only the problem of the competence of the governors, but a joint problem of the governing and the governed.

Other cross-national data show the existence of the phenomena of increasing demands for participation in Japan similar to those in West European and North American countries. Respondents in a poll were asked to choose the *two* most important values from among "law and order," "encouragement of more participation in vital political decisions," "restraint of the rise of prices," and "freedom of speech," values which were used in Professor Ronald Inglehart's (1971) six West European surveys.[4] Japanese respondents reacted in the following way: According to the margin-

[4]Japanese data were gathered by Kōmei Senkyo Renmei (Clean Election League) in a nationwide survey conducted in December 1972.

al distribution, "price restraint" was the first choice (70.4 percent), followed by "law and order" (45.3 percent), "participation" (35.1 percent), and "freedom of speech" (13.8 percent). The age and educational differences, however, were conspicuous. Among people in their twenties and those with university educations, "participation" surpassed "law and order" and gained the second ranking after "price restraint." In combinations of two values, the combination of "participation and free speech," which Professor Inglehart assumed to be the pure type of "postindustrial value," was less popular in Japan than in West European countries. Japanese responses were more concentrated in the intermediary "prices and participation" (Tables 1.2 and 1.3). Again, the younger and the better-educated clearly show their preference for the value of participation. (Among those in their twenties, about 15 percent prefer the combination of "participation and free speech," and, if coupled with "participation and prices," they are the top choices.)

The heightening of participatory motivation, however, is often related to increasing distrust of institutionalized channels of participation—that is, elections and political parties. Thus, the other side of the coin is the decline of political parties and the rise of various voluntary citizens' and residents' movements which dislike and refuse to follow the leadership of any political party and prefer protests instead of institutionalized participation. Respondents in a recent nationwide survey were asked the question: "Which would you prefer about the future of Japanese party politics—one, to back up a political party which can be relied on; two, to promote citizens' or residents' movements as they become necessary; three, to have nothing to do with political parties or politics at all?" Overall, 57 percent chose the first response, 17.3 percent the second, and 5.3 percent the third. Again, however, the younger (among those in their twenties, 22.4 percent prefer citizens' movements to parties and 6.5 percent are totally against politics) and the better-educated (23.1 percent of the university graduates prefer citizens' movements rather than political parties) place less trust in institutional channels of participation and are turning more to uninstitutional, protest-oriented movements (Kōmei Senkyo Renmei, 1974).

Protest-oriented movements have been spreading beyond the

Table 1.2: Japanese choice of combination of two values
            (percentage choosing each pair)

Order and prices	Order and free speech	Order and partici- pation	Prices and free speech	Prices and partici- pation	Free speech and partici- pation	Others	None D. K. N. A.
32.6	3.0	7.2	6.8	21.5	3.6	15.9	9.3 (N = 2,468)

Table 1.3: "Pure" value pairs by nations (percentage choosing each
            pair within given national sample)

Pair chosen:	Italy	France	Germany	Britain	Japan
Acquisitive	35	38	43	36	38
Postbourgeois	13	11	10	8	4

Source for data on Italy, France, Germany, and Britain: Inglehart, 1971.

younger and better-educated people and beyond urban and industrial areas to older, less-educated people and to local agricultural
and fishing areas. The *Mutsu*, the first Japanese nuclear-powered
test ship, drifted for fifty-four days because of the protests of the
fishermen of the bay in which the ship was based. There were
complicated reasons for this protest. Fear of nuclear accidents and
consequent possible contamination was certainly one. However,
the antipathy of the fishermen, living in the "periphery" and ill
treated by the "center" for a long time, toward the government
was reported to be another reason. Whatever the reasons, even
the fishermen in remote local areas were prepared to organize
protest movements when they felt the government was doing them
an injustice. Neither are farmers any longer silent and obedient
to the government whenever they feel they are treated unjustly.

If "governability" involves the capacity of the government
unilaterally to impose policies or plans that will affect the live-
lihoods of the citizens concerned, certainly such governability in
Japan has decreased. The Japanese government, however, because
of its long tradition of *Obrigkeit-staat*, often violates the usual standard of democracy in its behavior vis-à-vis citizens. In order to
emphasize democracy as well as governability, bureaucrats must
learn to be more careful and humane in doing their business.
Fortunately, Japanese bureaucrats—both national and local—
nowadays have such a learning capacity. Another factor which

has worked so far is the financial ability of government to afford additional spending in order to appease the protest movements by compensating for the alleged damage or promising costly changes in plans. It is certainly an easy solution, but one which will become more difficult in the approaching tighter governmental budget situation.

Social and Economic Values

In a society such as that of Japan after World War II, where indoctrination from above with the threat of punishment was nonexistent, where religious inhibitions after the separation of Shinto from the state were virtually nonexistent, and where social changes such as urbanization, increased income, and changes in consumption styles were so rapid, it would be natural to expect that every aspect of social relationships and the values underlying them would change considerably. Again, the most illuminating data showing the kinds of changes in social relations and their underlying values are found in the surveys conducted by the Institute of Mathematical Statistics, Ministry of Education, every five years since 1953. One question notes that "there are all sorts of attitudes toward life. Of those listed here (the list is shown), which one would you say comes closest to your feeling?" The percentages of those who picked "Don't think about money or fame, just live a life that suits your own tastes," have increased from 21 percent in 1953 to 27 percent in 1958, 30 percent in 1963, 32 percent in 1968, and 39 percent in 1973 by national average (ISM, 1974, p. 25). People have come to prefer less strenuous, more relaxed ways of life. The change has been most conspicuous among the younger generation.

What are the effects of such value changes on Japanese working behavior? Other survey data show that younger workers make stronger demands for shorter working hours, more holidays, and longer vacations, as well as for more opportunity for self-actualization on the job (Table 1.4).[5] However, the same table tells us about a number of other features of Japanese workers' demands: (1) Even among the young workers, wage raises are still the most

[5]Ministry of Labor, 1971, pp. 138–39.

Table 1.4: Demands raised by male workers (multiple answers, in percentages)

Age Item	-19	20-24	25-29	30-34	35-39	40-44	45-54	55-64	65-
Shorter working hours	49.0	42.5	37.1	34.6	32.3	29.6	24.5	28.8	30.4
More suitable job	19.9	24.4	23.7	17.4	17.3	14.5	14.4	14.9	10.4
Lifelong chance for improvement	12.7	16.4	15.6	15.0	11.9	10.3	9.9	6.3	7.2
Help for house-property building	12.2	17.5	23.7	27.9	27.5	26.4	22.7	20.2	15.2
Wage increase	63.8	63.1	65.7	66.9	67.8	65.9	60.8	51.7	42.4
Extension of retirement age	3.1	3.0	4.5	7.4	11.3	18.0	32.8	30.0	27.2
Welfare measures	14.0	15.3	12.0	12.5	10.9	9.9	9.4	18.1	33.6
Prevention of work accidents	13.1	8.9	8.0	8.4	10.6	13.4	14.7	14.2	12.8

outstanding demands. Money is not the goal of life, as the survey data show; however, wage increases are the gravest concern for workers at all ages. (2) Middle-aged people, especially those with growing families, have an increased desire to own a house, particularly on their own land, which will serve as security in an age of continued inflation. (3) Senior workers are naturally more concerned about their retirement, health care, and other welfare measures.

In spite of the changing values of the workers, the Japanese organizations—both governmental organizations and private enterprises—have so far maintained a high level of motivation for work among their employees, as indicated by a very low rate of absence (2.12 percent in a February 1973 survey).[6] The reasons for this success are: (1) The work force still contains a large proportion of older workers who are committed to older values of dedication to hard work and loyalty to their organizations. It is often pointed out that the middle-aged, middle-management people in

[6]From a survey on the illness and absence of workers conducted by the Ministry of Labor in February 1973. Vacations are counted as absences.

particular have a generational commitment of this kind. (2) Japanese big organizations with their paternalistic tradition have the capacity and resources to absorb a variety of demands from workers of various generations, including the youngest: better medical care, housing loans with lower interest, better recreational facilities, and, of course, so far, large annual increases in wages. Moreover, they are now introducing a five-day work week, longer vacations, and an extension of the retirement age from fifty-five to sixty; on these points, they are in a position to make concessions to workers' demands. (3) The Japanese younger generation is, in comparison with the previous, older generation, less work-oriented, less organization-oriented, and more self-assertive. In comparison with West European or American youth, however, the present Japanese youth still retains some traits favorable to the functioning of organizations if the organizations are clever enough to improve their operations. For instance, according to national character surveys, the preference of the Japanese for department chiefs who are paternalistic over those who are rationally specific remains unchanged (ISM, 1974, p. 55). Many of them want "self-actualization on the job." According to an eleven-country study of youth conducted by the Japanese government, the percentage of Japanese youths who have chosen "a job worth doing" as the most precious thing in their lives is the highest among the countries surveyed. In spite of signs of declining and less diffuse commitment to work organizations among Japanese youth, comparatively speaking, Japanese young people are still seeking more from the organizations, and, when organizations are flexible enough to appeal to self-assertive youth, they can maintain a fairly high level of work motivation, keeping the basic lines of Japanese organizations such as life employment, enterprise unions, diffuse social relationships within the organizations, and so on. For example, so far there has never even been serious discussion of abolishing the conveyor belt system in assembly lines in Japanese factories.

Labor and business specialists seem to agree that the Japanese organizational structure with its lifelong employment, enterprise unions, relatively strong commitment to the organization, and higher motivation to work will survive at least until 1980, as far as the internal factors within them are concerned (Ōkubo, 1972). Conversely, this means that in the first part of the 1980s Japan will reach the critical point where the accumulated changes in work ethics, attitudes toward life, and those toward company and union will necessitate corresponding changes in established labor relations, institutions, and practices. Therefore, it will be wiser for Japanese society to prepare for that period and preempt some of the anticipated reforms in advance.

Future Perspectives on Japanese Democracy

Japanese democracy seems to be suffering less from various changes which have already had threatening effects on democracies in other parts of the world. Japan seems to be enjoying a time lag between changes that have already occurred and the consequences to follow, partly due to its remaining reservoir of traditional values and partly due to the structure of its economy.[7] Some of the consequences of these changes have, however, already weakened the leadership capacity of Japanese democracy, and the world has been demanding more positive action of Japan, which can be generated only by a higher level of leadership.

The LDP is facing the possibility of losing its majority position in the Diet. The opposition parties are split, and there is no opposition party that can take the responsibility of governing by itself. Of course, a multiparty system and coalition formation are not intrinsically dysfunctional in the operation of democracy. On the other hand, since coalition formation is quite a new experience to Japanese politics on the national level, some confusion would be unavoidable. In foreign policy decision making, any

[7]Since the 1973–74 oil crisis, many observers have argued for a return to traditional values. For instance, the ex-Vice Minister of MITI, Yamashita Eimei, replied in a *Newsweek* interview as follows: Question: "What about the impact of Japan's economic crunch on traditional values?" Answer: "I see it as leading to a return to traditional values rather than a departure from them. During the past decade, Japanese youth abandoned all ideas of saving. They spent lavishly on clothes, electronics, and cars. But since the oil crisis, we have returned to more basic Japanese concepts. I don't think we will revert entirely to the mentality of Tokugawa feudalism, but we will be able to strike a happy balance" (*Newsweek*, November 18, 1974, p. 15).

coalition—even the most moderate one of the LDP and the Democratic Socialists—will bring with it a weakening of the Japan-U.S. alliance to some degree and a more drifting (or flexible) foreign policy than that under the LDP's single rule. Domestically, a multiparty system and coalition formation are good for interest articulation but not necessarily good for interest aggregation. Under the LDP's single rule, pressure groups have succeeded in getting shares in the government budget. Any coalition will be exposed to more diverse pressures in budget making and policy formation.

The Increasing Importance of Urban, Educated Nonpartisans

In the mid-1960s, the Socialists seemed to have a bright future, with a good chance of replacing the LDP and taking the position of governing party at some point. The Socialists were then getting the support of the better-educated voters in the urban areas (see Chapter 5). Today, however, in the urban areas, not only the LDP, but also the Socialist Party is declining in influence. The Kōmei, the Communists, and, to a lesser degree, the Democratic Socialists are getting a larger share of the votes than before. But these parties are also uncertain about their futures because what exists in big cities is a vast number of voters with a nonpartisan orientation, whose educational level is high. It seems that no single party will be able to organize this section of the voters as a solid basis of support. Fortunately, the possibility is quite slim or nonexistent that these people will come to support the extreme rightists or extreme leftists, even in the case of a sudden international or domestic crisis. But they are unpredictable in voting, switching their votes from one party to another, and they like to vote for a popular nonpartisan candidate if such a candidate can be found. Successful candidates in gubernatorial elections or mayoral elections in urban areas are those who can appeal to this kind of voter in addition to gaining the support of more than one party. The increasing importance of urban, educated nonpartisans has made politicians and political parties more responsive to the demands of the populace outside their regular supporters. However, by encouraging excessive populist responsiveness in politicians and political parties, it can also lower their capacity for leadership.

The Japan Communist Party (JCP) has been successful in recent elections in increasing its vote totals and number of seats at both the national and local levels. To take the case of the House of Representatives, the JCP's votes have increased from 2.2 million votes (4.76 percent of the total votes cast) in 1967 to 3.2 million votes (6.81 percent) in 1969, and to 5.5 million votes (10.49 percent) in 1972. Especially in metropolitan areas, the JCP is now getting about 20 percent of the total vote. The JCP has more than 300,000 members (virtually the largest solid party membership in Japan), and its daily party newspaper has more than a two-million circulation. A number of prefectural governors and big-city mayors were elected with the joint support of the JCP and the Socialists (and, in some cases, the Kōmei Party).

Does the JCP present any possible threat to Japanese democracy in the near future? Most of the observations seem to support the negative (that is, optimistic) answer, for the following reasons. First, the JCP seems to be approaching its limit in terms of share of the votes. As a matter of fact, in the 1976 general election for the House of Representatives, JCP's votes stagnated on the level of 10 percent as a nationwide average and 24.4 percent in the first electoral district of Kyoto as the best record. Second, a major factor which has contributed to the increased support for the JCP is its soft and flexible domestic policies combined with nationalistic foreign policies independent of the Soviet and Chinese communist parties. Many domestic issues would be negotiable with this kind of JCP. In the foreign policy area, however, an independent and nationalistic JCP would increase Japan's isolation, not only from the United States but also from China and other Asian countries. In this respect, it can be said that the JCP would work dysfunctionally.

Japanese democracy is not in a serious crisis at the present moment. However, the time lag mentioned above means that Japanese democracy will face the consequences of social changes in a future, possibly tighter situation. In comparison with the United States, where the "democratic surge" can be regarded as already having passed its peak, in Japan there is no sign of decline in the increasing tide of popular demands. On the other hand, the financial resources of the government are showing signs of stagnation. The reservoir of traditional values of obedience, groupism, frugality, etc., which are still working to counterbalance the rising tide of popular demands and protest, might be exhausted at some future time. Thus, the time-lagged consequences of change and the exhaustion of the traditional reservoir will both come in the early 1980s, as many people argue.

What will become of Japanese democracy after 1980? According to a survey on national goals, a majority of the Japanese leaders surveyed believe that Japan will continue to be committed to democratic principles and to a "uniquely Japanese democracy" in the future (Tanaka, 1974). But what this would look like and how it can be built are still unclear.

Chapter 2
Democracy in Japan since 1945

In spite of the fears of a "revival of Japanese militarism" expressed by critics both in Japan and abroad, Japanese democracy seems to have been consolidated during the thirty years since Japan's defeat in World War II. Of course, like the democracies in North America and Western Europe, Japanese democracy has many problems which must be dealt with if it is to survive and develop. Moreover, if some kind of grave emergency should strike these democracies in North America, Western Europe, or Japan, there is no absolute guarantee that the form of liberal democracy found in these countries at present would continue to exist. However, I am not going to discuss these future possibilities here; rather, I will examine the thus-far-successful case of postwar Japanese democracy in order to shed light on some theoretical models of political development.

Establishment of Japanese Democracy after World War II

The institutions of Japanese democracy after World War II were formed under the Allied Occupation, the leadership of which was in the hands of the Americans. However, in spite of the apparent imposition of democratic reforms by the Occupation forces, by and large those reforms were congruent with, or at least not contradictory to, the reform potential within Japanese society. The U.S.-made draft of the Constitution had many points in common with a draft proposed by Japanese liberals; and many other reforms, although initiated by the Supreme Commander for the Allied Powers (SCAP), were also in the direction proposed by liberal critics

43

(in the case of reform of the family code and the educational system) or even by bureaucrats (in the case of land reform) in prewar days. In other words, the tradition and accumulated potential of Japanese liberalism, as expressed by what is called Taishō democracy[1] and enlightened bureaucrats, provided the background and the tools for reform under the Occupation. Postwar reforms were the synthesis of internally accumulated reform potentials and external pressure from the American Occupation forces.

Or, if we use Dahl's (1971) model of polyarchy, the level of participation in Japan's political system had been increased to such a level that it was prepared to move to polyarchy once obstacles to liberalization were removed. Inspired by Dahl's model, Shinohara and Miyazaki (1974, pp. 242–44) made the following comments concerning the historical development of democracy in Japan:

> After the Meiji Restoration, Japan experienced two big movements for democracy. One was, needless to say, the Freedom and Popular Rights movement,[2] and another was the Taishō democracy movement. . . .By the Freedom and Popular Rights movement and the promulgation of the Meiji Constitution, Japan had begun to "take off" from premodern society. . . . After the Russo-Japanese War, a new era of change had begun. . . . The Taishō democracy movement enhanced this tendency for change. This movement had two aspects. One was indicated by the *minponshugi* movement led by Yoshino Sakuzō, aiming toward the democratic reform of constitutional government and the enhancement of party government, and the other was represented by the movement led by Yamakawa Hitoshi, aiming at the establishment and the recognition of *musan seitō* (party for the propertyless). In other words, the Taishō democracy movement promoting democracy and socialism tried to raise the level of participation and public contestation at once. Actually, these aims were partially achieved in universal

[1]Taishō is the reign period of the Taishō emperor (1912–26), when a democratic movement emerged and certain democratic reforms were achieved under the Meiji Constitution. Taishō democracy began with the inauguration of the Hara Cabinet in 1918, and its democratic practices were somehow maintained throughout the 1920s.

[2]This movement began in 1873 and lasted until 1890, when the Diet was finally inaugurated.

manhood suffrage (1925) and the recognition which allowed somehow the existence of the socialist parties. In this sense, in this era of Taishō democracy, one can say that Japanese politics entered into the stage of "near polyarchy." However, as is well known, in the same year of 1925 when universal manhood suffrage was introduced, the Public Security Maintenance Law was promulgated. This fact clearly shows that Japanese politics had the characteristics of being rather flexible towards participation but very repressive of public contestation. . . . Moreover, Taishō democracy had a number of vulnerable points, such as the *genrō* system, the House of Peers, and the military, and finally collapsed into dictatorship or "inclusive hegemony." . . . However, after many years of regression, through the post–World War II reforms, Japan finally—or, more precisely speaking, suddenly—has entered into the stage of polyarchy.

"Counter-Course" and Stabilization in the 1950s and 1960s

The U.S. Occupation of Japan ended on April 28, 1952, when the Peace Treaty between Japan and most of the Allies came into effect. With the end of the Occupation, the Japanese government and the governing party—at that time two conservative parties, the Liberal Party and the Reformist Party (Kaishin-tō); after their amalgamation in 1955, they became the Liberal Democratic Party—regained the freedom to make sovereign political decisions. There were moves by the conservatives to revise the "excessive" reforms initiated under the Occupation. The right wings of the conservative parties wanted a less liberal, prewar-type regime. These moves by the conservatives in the 1950s just after the end of the U.S. Occupation were called a "counter-course." At that time, a prominent Japanese political scientist, Tsuji Kiyoaki, commented on these moves, distinguishing between "natural reaction" and "political reaction" to the reforms introduced during the Occupation period, meaning by the former some readjustment of reforms introduced in Occupation days for technical reasons and by the latter reversion to prewar-type institutions and practices (Tsuji, 1952). He thought that there were good reasons for the natural reaction and that it could contribute to the development of democracy in Japan. However, he expressed his grave concern that if the political reaction should be successful, it would cause a serious disturbance to the development of democracy in Japan.

Professor Tsuji's concern proved to be excessive. By and large, the postwar reforms were kept intact, and Japanese democracy survived the counter-course movement of the 1950s. The reasons for its survival deserve attention. In the first place, taking advantage of the already introduced polyarchical system, the Japanese opposition parties—especially the Japan Socialist Party—were able to prevent the actualization of counter-course moves by the Conservatives. According to a stipulation of the Constitution of 1947, revision of the Constitution requires two-thirds approval of both Houses of the Diet and referendum approval. Although the conservatives had a majority of the seats in both Houses during the 1950s, they failed to have the two-thirds of the seats in the Diet necessary to initiate a move to revise the Constitution. But wasn't it possible for the conservatives—or their rightist faction—to overcome such obstacles? This kind of thing has happened many times in other countries. The Republic of Korea has had this experience. So the next question to be asked in the Japanese case is why such attempts have not occurred.

One possible answer is the pay-off explanation—in other words, the relationship between the cost of repression and the cost of tolerance. Cost-benefit analysis is always tricky, both because the cost is always relative to the benefit or the loss and because it always involves subjective perception and evaluation. In the presence of external threats and/or internal difficulties for a particular political system, the costs of tolerance will outweigh the benefits. We see a typical case at the present moment in South Korea (Republic of Korea). President Park Chung Hee firmly believes that the threat from the North (Democratic People's Republic of Korea) is so imminent and the internal tasks of the South (Republic of Korea) are so vast that his country cannot afford the luxury of liberal democracy. And the Korean people are at least partially persuaded by his logic.

For the Japanese conservatives in the 1950s, even for the far rightists among them, the cost of repression seemed too high to allow them to take bold repressive measures. Japan was lucky in the sense that it was exempt from serious external threat by its geographical isolation and by the U.S. defense umbrella. As for internal difficulties, Japan was without internal ethnic conflict because it had been essentially a highly homogeneous nation and without major economic difficulties; it prospered because of the increased demand generated first by the Korean War and later by its own economic capacity. The Japanese conservatives had no reason to resort to violent action because, in spite of their belief that things should be run more in the prewar style, the *status quo* functioned well.

Later, in the 1960s, rapid economic growth brought with it socioeconomic changes which were more congruent with postwar democracy. Economic growth created a huge market for labor in which young people could easily find jobs. Moreover, demand for young labor power so surpassed the supply that wages for the young improved rapidly. Thus, the young people became more independent from their parents and moved freely from their home towns into big cities or industrial areas. This kind of independence was more congruent with the postwar reformed family code than with the prewar type of paternalistic family code. During the 1950s, whenever the conservatives talked about correcting excessive postwar reforms, the revision of the family code was a favorite topic. However, since the early 1960s, they have ceased to raise the subject.

The Need for Continuous Consolidation

Japan after World War II succeeded in establishing and consolidating its democratic, polyarchical regime, aided by the existence of reform potential, the emergence of opposition parties which strove to maintain the postwar reforms, lack of serious external threats, and economic prosperity. However, consolidation doesn't mean perfection. A number of problems are besetting Japanese polyarchy. First of all, Japanese polyarchy tends to accommodate participation more easily than it does opposition. It has been so historically and it is still so today. Therefore, Japanese democracy has been criticized on the one hand for its insufficient level of liberality and its intolerance of opposition, and on the other hand for overconformity and social particularism. One is tempted to speak about the nature of Japanese political culture and Japanese behavior patterns in general (see Nakane, 1967).

Another kind of problem is a new one. As is often pointed out, since the late 1960s, in both Western Europe, North America, and Japan, there has emerged a heightened wave of participation and contestation. Based on a survey conducted in Western European countries, Inglehart (1971) has pointed out the emergence of postindustrial values which emphasize nonmaterial values such as freedom, independence, and participation. A number of signs indicate the emergence and spread of such values in the U.S., Canada, and Japan, too. Ordinary citizens have greatly increased their demands for participation and contestation in recent years. We have to look into the viability of a new polyarchy which can accommodate these rapidly growing demands for participation and contestation. We don't yet know much about this "new polyarchy." But it seems likely that it will have to accommodate a large number of demands for participation and contestation in ways less institutionalized than before.

Chapter 3
Consequences of Economic Growth

The changes in Japan's economy over the past fifteen years have been vast. For example, the percentage of the population engaged in agriculture dropped from 40 percent in 1955 to 19 percent in 1970, and the GNP increased from $25 billion to roughly $200 billion in the same period, but the impact of these changes on Japan's society and politics is still to be seen.

Generally speaking, the greatest impact has been felt on the style of consumption. Ownership of television sets, washing machines, and refrigerators has increased dramatically. By 1965 over 90 percent of all Japanese households owned black-and-white television sets. By 1970 most also owned washing machines, and refrigerators lagged only slightly behind. Then, just as the distribution of these three products was reaching a near saturation point, sales promoters and journalists began to herald a new wave of consumer demands, this time for the "three c's": a color television, an air conditioner, and a car. Taste in food also has changed: the Japanese today eat less rice and more meat, eggs, and fruits.

Such changes in consumption style have occurred not only in cities, but also in rural areas. Although the rural population has declined in size, it has not declined in income. In fact, rural income has kept pace with and in some cases surpassed that of urban dwellers. This has been due in part to protective measures taken by the government, which has guaranteed the price of rice, provided subsidies for improving agricultural facilities, and maintained a high tariff on agricultural products from abroad. It is explained also by the increased demand for seasonal labor, especially in the construction industry, which provides opportunities for farmers to earn a cash income during off seasons. Thus the

49

homogenization of consumption styles has become conspicuous throughout Japan.

This new style has been colored particularly by the rise in the economic status of youth. Since long before World War II Japanese employment had been characterized by a wage and promotion system based on seniority and a preference for lifelong employment (see Abegglen, 1958). These characteristics survived the reforms of the postwar period, in some ways becoming more deeply ingrained than before. In the late 1960s, however, a labor shortage developed. Young people, whose average wage was far lower than that of their seniors, were quick to press for higher wages. As a result, wages for young workers have begun to rise more rapidly than those for senior workers. In addition, opportunities for part-time jobs for university students have increased. Thus the purchasing power of young people has increased and a vast youth market for consumer goods has been formed. Shrewd businessmen have taken advantage of this change, catering to a new youth taste throughout the country. The "three c's" are being accompanied by miniskirts, leather boots, blue jeans, maxicoats, bowling alleys, midnight snack bars, and weekend ski resorts.

The recent experience of Japan, like that of Europe and the United States, would seem to demonstrate that where there is a significant increase in personal income, a freewheeling private enterprise system, and no strong state, religious, or other inhibitions on taste, the outward style of a people's life can be changed in a short period of time indeed. But what of the inner life, the world of the mind where values reign? Have the great changes in Japan's economy exerted a similarly strong impact on this realm as well? Does a young Japanese man in his colorful shirt and wide tie or a young Japanese woman in her miniskirt and leather boots think at all like an American or West European youth with similar consumer tastes? Or underneath these new styles does the young Japanese still share the values of the older generation?

One would expect of course that the value system and the frame of reference of a people would change to some extent in a situation like that of postwar Japan where no official efforts at indoctrination have been made and no strong religious inhibitions have been operative; but the experience of Japan is that even under such conditions, the values of a people change rather slowly and they change differentially with the generations. There has been a time lag between the diffusion of the new consumption style in Japan and the spread of new values congruent with this style. A gap also has opened between the generations, the young being readier than the old to accept both the new style and the new values associated with it.

Since 1953 the Institute of Statistical Mathematics in Tokyo has conducted a nationwide survey of Japanese national character every five years, using many of the same questions (Sakamoto, 1974). A comparison of the answers obtained in successive surveys shows that over this period some values have changed and some have not. Apparently there has been a slow but steady decline in such traditional values, for example, as the importance of family continuity, devotion to the Shinto cult, and respect for political leaders. On the other hand, such an attitude as preference for a paternalistic supervisor, so different from American attitudes, appears to show no change over time or between the generations.

This attitude, however, seems to be exceptional. Most attitudes showing change also show a remarkable age differential, and the marginal change in the time series suggests that the new attitudes will continue to spread more and more as the present young generation grows older and new generations come on the scene. A typical example of this is the growing attitude that one should live one's life "to suit one's own taste."[1] The percentage of people in their early twenties (20–24 years old) who express this attitude has steadily increased from 32 percent in 1953 to 38 percent in 1958, to 44 percent in 1963, to 52 percent in 1968. If we simply extrapolate this trend into the future, by 1980 it may be expected that an overwhelming proportion of young people will share this conception; and if we dare to use this as an indicator of post-industrial values, it would appear that postindustrial values may well predominate in Japanese society in the near future.

Additional data indicate that another attitudinal trend has begun to take shape in recent years, one connected with the en-

[1]This question was originally designed in 1930. It was used in surveys of 20-year-old male conscripts in 1930 and 1940. To secure a time-series comparison, the Institute of Statistical Mathematics asked the question again in 1953 and has been asking it in repeated surveys since then.

Table 3.1:   Preferences of the Japanese people (in percentages)

"Among the following, which do you think the most important to you?"	
Life and health	47.0
Family	21.2
Love and friendship	9.8
Nation, society, and politics	6.4
Work and trust	5.3
Children	5.2
Money and wealth	2.6
"Which do you think more important?"	
Preservation of nature	59.7
Development (*e.g.*, construction of roads, housing sites and factories)	20.2
"Which of the following would you prefer?"	
Increase of income	43.3
Shortening of work hours	16.2
Can't choose (implies welcoming of shortened working hours on the condition that level of income is guaranteed)	33.1

Source: Keizai Shingikai Kokuminsenkōdo Chōsa Iinkai (1972). The survey was conducted in May 1972 among a 14,120 sample of the Japanese population over 15 years of age.

vironment. Air and water pollution and other environmental destruction caused by the economic growth of the 1960s has come suddenly to be highlighted by the mass media. Movements against pollution and environmental destruction have erupted in various industrial zones where residents up to now had tolerated the sufferings caused by industrial pollution in the belief that pollution was a necessary by-product of industry and that the prosperity of the industrial enterprise was essential to that of the community and the individual. But postindustrial values are evident in the results of a survey conducted in 1972 in which health and life are preferred to money and wealth, and nature to economic development (see Table 3.1). However, people are still very much concerned with their incomes; the same survey shows that a larger income is more desired than a shorter workweek and indeed that a shorter workweek is desired by most only if income is not affected. It is apparent, therefore, that "industrial values," emphasizing income and work, remain strong. Furthermore, such traditional values as the preference for a paternalistic supervisor are still cherished by many. Thus, among the Japanese people today, three value systems have come to coexist: traditional, industrial, and postindustrial.

The question we now turn to is, How are these value systems reflected in politics? First of all, let us look into the people's preferences for each of the political parties, and see how this affects the total pattern of politics through elections and the consequent distribution of seats in the Diet.

We have seen that over the past decade there has been a shift in the value structure away from those attitudes imbued with tradition and even those fostered by the industrial society of the recent past, and toward those more congruent with the postindustrial order now emerging. One might suppose therefore that this would be reflected in a similar shift in voter allegiance away from the more conservative and toward the more reformist parties. Such indeed was the expectation of most observers of the Japanese scene in the mid-1960s. The emergence of postindustrial values was not then foreseen, but the cleavage of Japanese society between traditionalists and modernists was everywhere apparent. In these circumstances, Japanese politics seemed best understood as "cultural politics"—that is, as a competition for power between tradition-oriented groups, who supported the Liberal Democratic Party (LDP), and the "modern" sectors of society, who supported the opposition parties. From this perspective, since the modern sectors of society were gaining steadily at the expense of the traditional sectors, it seemed reasonable to expect within the foreseeable future that a fundamental political change would take place: the conservative party would be voted out and a new and powerful coalition of socialist-led reformist forces would come to power.

The concept of cultural politics was not wholly wrong. In 1972 as in 1960, it was the tradition-oriented groups—farmers, fishermen, merchants, small manufacturers, the less highly educated, and older people—who supported the conservative party most strongly. In contrast, the modern sectors of the population—white-collar workers, manual workers, the more highly educated, and the young (when they voted)—still preferred the oppoittion parties. This evidence is supported by the results of a survey conducted in 1972 which show that the correlation between holders of traditional values and supporters of the LDP is still fairly high (see Chapter 9).

Moreover, as the proportion of the tradition-oriented groups in society declined, so did the strength of the conservative party. By

Table 3.2:   Correlation between occupation, age, educational level, and party
support, 1971

	Occupation	Age	Educational level
Rural area (*gunbu*)	0.470	0.227	0.140
Small cities	0.460	0.260	0.181
Middle cities	0.477	0.251	0.046
Seven big cities	0.287	0.114	0.124
Setagaya ward in Tokyo	0.129	0.095	0.114

Note: Figures for the upper four rows are computed from the original data in the
survey made by Kōmei Senkyo Renmei at the time of the 1971 House of Councillors
election. The figures are square roots of Crammer's contingency coefficients. Party
support is regrouped into two categories: LDP vs. JSP, DSP, and JCP.

1972, for example, popular support for the LDP had dropped
to 46.9 percent from 63.2 percent in 1955. This drop reflected the
decline in the proportion of farmers among the Japanese working
force from 40 percent to 19 percent over the same period. Contrary
to expectations, however, the LDP drop did not reflect it exactly.
Conservative strength has held up better than expected, and after
a decade of fundamental changes in the socioeconomic structure
of the country, the Liberal Democrats remain in power.

There would seem to be three reasons for this turn of events.
Since 1960, the number of persons who are reluctant to name the
party whose candidate they have supported has grown. Another
development may be related to this: if one breaks down the data
on the socioeconomic bases of party support according to the size
of community, one discovers that the more highly urbanized the
environment, the less salient are age, education level, and occupation as determining factors of party support (see Table 3.2). Since
the urban sector of Japan has expanded strikingly in recent years,
these facts suggest a decline in party loyalty and a possible increase
in the floating vote. A second explanation is to be found in the fact
that certain of the modern groups, especially the young and
the highly educated, are showing an increasing propensity not to
vote at all, thereby weakening proportionately the reformist parties. This nonvoting tendency would seem to be related to the
spread of certain postindustrial values exemplified by the preference for living one's life "to suit one's taste."

But perhaps the single most important explanation for the continued strength of the LDP and the growth in importance of the

Kōmei and Communist Parties is the growing strength of organization in those parties and the relative weakness of such organization in the Japan Socialist Party (JSP) and the Democratic Socialist Party (DSP). The traditional parties in Japan, true to their nineteenth-century origins, were organizations of officeholders and local notables, having little or no mass base. After World War II, these loose elitist groups, which had their counterparts in the traditional order, were challenged by more highly organized parties that sought mass membership on the model of the socialist and Marxist-Leninist parties of the West. The Japan Communist Party went farthest along this path and is today the most highly organized of all Japanese parties, increasing its dues-paying membership from about 20,000 in 1955 to 300,000 today and building up its daily party newspaper distribution to more than two million copies (Tawara, 1972, p. 17–28).

All other parties have felt the magnetism of this model, but none has been able to duplicate it. Memberships in the Japan Socialist Party and the Democratic Socialist Party remain extremely low (35,000 and 50,000 respectively).[2] For organizational strength they have come to rely, somewhat in the manner of the British Labour Party, on what Maurice Duverger (1964, pp. 5–16) calls "indirect structures"—that is, on two national federations of labor unions, the JSP on Sōhyō with its 4.5 million members and the DSP on Dōmei with its 2.2 million members. The Kōmei Party has another kind of indirect structure, the Sōka Gakkai (Value Creation Society), which is a lay association of the Nichiren Shōshū Buddhist sect with five million members.[3]

Among the conservatives the response to the need for stable party support has taken a different form, that of building kōenkai, not for the Liberal Democratic Party as such, but for each individual conservative politician in his own district. Since the formation of the party in 1955 the number of kōenkai has grown dramatically until now they are estimated to embrace about 17.2 percent of the party's supporters or about 4.5 million people and to have

[2]As of August 1971. From Yomiuri nenkan (Yomiuri Yearbook), 1972.
[3]Sōka Gakkai itself boasts that it has 7.5 million households as its members. However, outside observers and analysts agree that this is an inflated figure. According to the common understanding among them, a membership of 4 or 5 million would be closer to the reality. See White (1970, pp. 57–61).

contacted possibly 20 or 30 million more (Kōmei Senkyo Renmei, 1972, p. 206). Through such associations, the conservative politicians now gather and distribute benefits, the latter ranging from the soliciting of governmental funds for local public works to arranging for university admissions or jobs for children of constituents. The *kōenkai* serve social and recreational functions too: they organize sightseeing tours, for example, and sponsor bowling matches. The interesting thing is that these organizations do not resemble mass parties of the West European type; there is, for example, no clear definition of membership and no clear concentration on issues, the organizational principle being personal loyalty to the particular politician concerned (see Curtis, 1971, ch. 5). In this latter regard they are distinguished also from the American-type party in which affiliation, loose though it is, in most cases survives a change in leadership. It has been suggested that the relationship between an LDP politician and his *kōenkai* members is similar to the patron-client relationship found in groups in developing societies (Scott, 1972). But the *kōenkai* often includes a vast number of people under its umbrella, the largest reportedly embracing about 100,000 persons; moreover, the relationship between the politician and the *kōenkai* members is more tenuous and organizational than one usually finds in groups in developing societies. If this is clientelism, it is organizational clientelism.

The growth of these peculiarly Japanese forms of political organization, generating as they do intense competition within the party, has been condemned by the LDP's central leadership almost from the beginning. In 1963, for example, these organizations were severely faulted for "concentrating on activities centered on particular individuals and hindering activities of the party."[4] The solution, it was felt, was gradually to absorb them into the party organization, in the beginning by requiring that influential members and at least 500 members of each be registered in local branches of the party. The effort was made and by the summer of 1971, 800,000 persons from the local sponsoring associations were reported to have been registered. But the results have been disappointing. Once registered, few remained in the party to pay their dues for even an additional year. The reason

[4]Proposals by the Subcommittee on Organization, October 15, 1963.

seems to have been that the lists of 500 persons from each personal sponsoring association were often drawn up without the consent of the persons involved, and the dues for the first year were usually paid by the politician concerned, not by the *kōenkai* members.

Not only have the conservative *kōenkai* not been absorbed into the LDP, but their strength is growing. According to recent surveys, the percentage of the electorate who acknowledge membership in a *kōenkai* rose from 5.8 percent in 1967 to 11.5 percent in 1970, to 13.7 percent in 1971.

Thus, except for the Japan Communist Party, the highly organized mass party which so caught the imagination of many Japanese during the industrial era never actually caught on. The Socialists remain dependent on their unions, and efforts to encourage labor union members to affiliate directly with the party have usually resulted in the addition of "sleeping members" who nominally register but drop out within a year or two. The Kōmei Party, which in 1970 separated itself from its own "indirect structure," the Sōka Gakkai, found it could attract very few members who were not from the Gakkai. Without the direct backup of the Gakkai as in the past, it suffered a striking defeat in the December 1972 election. And the Liberal Democratic Party is more and more dependent on its personal sponsoring associations. Clearly, Japan's traditional paternalistic behavior patterns and values proved to be remarkably adaptable to the demands generated by industrial society, and there is every reason to believe that they will survive in the politics of the postindustrial age.

On the other hand, the emergence of certain postindustrial values also is not without effect. Citizen participation, for example, has been more and more highly valued. The result has not been the reinvigoration of existing political parties, but the emergence of nonpartisan citizens' movements around such issues as environmental protection, educational improvement, and the promotion of welfare. Local governments have been more susceptible than the central government to such demands. As a matter of fact, a political style emphasizing citizen participation has become more and more popular among the candidates running for the office of governor or mayor. Recently in local elections, especially in big cities, candidates supported by the LDP who emphasize the importance of their ties with the governing party and the central government have been losing by unexpectedly large margins to candidates backed by the opposition parties who emphasize the importance of citizen participation. A good example is Minobe Ryōkichi's gubernatorial election campaign in Tokyo in 1971.

Another recent change is the increasing importance of the personalities of the candidates. Of course, personality has always counted in Japanese elections; however, recently fluctuation in the votes according to the attractiveness of the candidates has become particularly pronounced. The electoral success of Minobe is at least partly attributable to his famous smile and dynamic personality.

The persistence of older values and structures side by side with new forms of political participation and the new appeals of political candidates makes prediction of the future of Japanese politics very uncertain. The LDP may lose its majority in the House of Councillors at any time. The Communists, in turn, may be able to continue their advance, possibly securing 10 percent of the votes and seats and acquiring thereby the capability of creating more noisy parliamentary sessions and even of paralyzing the Diet. But what would follow if the LDP should lose its majority in the Diet—which party would benefit most or which parties or factions would form the succeeding coalition—is impossible to foresee.

The impact of postindustrialism on the bureaucracy is also ambiguous. On the one hand, it would seem to strengthen the bureaucracy. In spite of the postwar reforms under the Occupation, the Japanese bureaucracy, especially in comparison with that in the United States, has remained strongly centralized and powerful. These characteristics give it an advantage in utilizing improved informational technology for elaborate and sophisticated planning. The Japanese bureaucracy has long been able to get meticulous statistical data from local bodies simply by circulating orders or notices. Now various ministries of the central government are introducing high-level technology for storing and retrieving the data thus gathered. The Ministry of Labor, for example, as early as 1964 established a huge computerized center for the labor market, capable of storing and retrieving the information gathered from labor stabilization offices throughout the country. The Ministry of Construction is trying to establish a territorial information center, where detailed information on regional development all over Japan will be stored and retrieved.

The bureaucracy was strengthened also by the expansion of the national budget, made possible by the growth of the economy and the concomitant "natural increase" of governmental revenues through taxes. While the GNP was doubling every five years, the governmental budget also doubled every five years, growing eightfold between 1955 and 1970. Of course, the budget is determined by the Diet; however, it is the bureaucrats who draft the budget and the bureaucrats who administer the ever-growing expenditures.

One of the reasons for the bureaucracy's ability to adapt to the new postindustrial forces has been the existence of an elite corps within it. By "elite corps" I mean not only those who are presently occupying top positions in the bureaucracy, but also those junior bureaucrats who have passed certain categories of higher civil service examinations. They exist as a semiformally recognized group with high solidarity and interaction within each ministry. The practice is to give them fast promotion and careful training. Although recruitment is based on open examination, the number of annual recruits is carefully limited. For instance, in the Ministry of International Trade and Industry, with 12,000 personnel, around twenty new graduates from the universities are accepted annually as new members of its elite corps, which numbers about 400 or so. Early selection, careful training, planned rotation, and fast promotion work in general to maintain a high capability and morale.

But the future of the bureaucracy is no more certain than that of the parties, for other forces are at work to weaken and change it. For one thing, its present position rests in part on close cooperation with the LDP majority in the Diet. If this majority should be replaced by a multiparty coalition, one result might be political immobility and a clear opportunity for the bureaucracy to gain more influence as an independent, stabilizing power; but, alternatively, it is also possible that in such a circumstance the various partners of the coalition would approach the bureaucracy separately and competitively, causing it to lose the unity fostered hitherto by close association with the LDP.

Second, it may be challenged by increasing local initiative. The emerging emphasis on participatory values has been felt especially in urban and suburban areas. As mentioned above, the successful gubernatorial or mayoral candidates are often those who encourage citizen participation and demand more decentralization of governmental power. Under these new leaders, local governments tend to follow a different line from that of the national government. Thus, even if the LDP were able to maintain its majority in the Diet and even if the national bureaucracy were able to retain its powerful position at the center, an emerging friction between the national and local governments may well operate to counter the bureaucracy's centralized and sophisticated planning from above. Thus the triangle of the LDP, bureaucracy, and big business which has been so powerful up to now may in the future meet more and more resistance from a loose tripartite coalition of opposition parties, urban local governments, and citizens' movements—a counterforce which might gain particular strength should the LDP lose its majority in the Diet.

Third, it may be doubted whether the elite corps of the Japanese national bureaucracy can survive as presently constituted. The discriminatory system on which the elite corps is based may shortly find itself in difficulty. So far, the bureaucracy has successfully limited the recruitment of university graduates to the elite corps, filling the bulk of its nonelite jobs with older persons and female high school graduates. Were this practice to continue, it would result in the lowering of the quality of the nonelite sector of the national bureaucracy. In any event, with the spread of higher education, the pressure is on for the national bureaucracy to accept a far larger number of university graduates than has been its practice. If this change is made, university graduates will need to be appointed to what have been thought of as nonelite as well as elite positions, making it increasingly difficult to preserve the uniqueness of the elite corps. The solution for this would seem to be to open the gate wide to university graduates and let them compete on the job. Actually, local governments are already doing this; for instance, the Tokyo metropolitan government alone has been hiring more university graduates annually than the total number recruited annually for the elite corps of the entire national bureaucracy. The present elite corps, of course, is reluctant to make a reform which would result in the dissolution of its privileged status and the loss of its special training, with the possible effect of lowering the bureaucracy's effectiveness. The LDP also is opposed since it is fused with the elite corps through personal ties and the mutual exchange of benefits. But the time is not far distant when such a reform will have to be considered, either because of pressure from other political parties with which the LDP is forced to bargain to form a coalition or because of acute labor unrest provoked by the present discriminatory system.

Why, in comparison with the speed and the scale of change in Japan's economy and consumption style, have changes in the political sphere been so gradual? The truth is that not only in politics, but in all areas of society which are deeply imbued with norms and values, changes do not come quickly unless there has been forced indoctrination or brainwashing. The widespread acceptance of new values usually requires a generational change. Meanwhile, old values persist. It should not be surprising, therefore, that in Japan, where 40 percent of the people were engaged in agriculture as late as 1955, traditional communal values nourished in the agrarian village remain strong.

Accordingly, just as Japan was a latecomer to the industrial age, so will it be later than the United States and West European countries in fully entering the period of postindustrialization. With the passing of time, gradually the traditional and industrial values will be more and more sloughed off and postindustrial values will in the main takeover; and only sometime later will the politics of Japan come gradually to resemble the politics of other postindustrial societies in Western Europe and the United States.

But this resemblance is apt to be not only slow in coming but in the end incomplete. One must recognize the viable nature of certain Japanese traditional norms and values and the dexterity of the Japanese elites in utilizing them, as they did, for nation-building and industrialization in the prewar period and for reconstruction and economic growth in the postwar period. Life-long employment and the seniority wage system, for example, are still being practiced even after the rise of fairly strong labor unions. *Ringisei*, often translated as "decision making from below" or "consensus decision making," is an established practice in Japanese organizational decision making, in which the plans are drawn up by the middle echelon and circulated upward successively through the hierarchy of the organization for approval. *Nemawashi* is the practice of informal consultation to get the approval of the people concerned in advance of presenting a formal proposal (Tsuji, 1968). These and other practices, the origins of which can be traced far back in traditional Japanese cultural patterns, still survive and function in the most modern Japanese private enterprise or governmental bureaucracy. In the political sphere, LDP politicians have built up expensive but effective political vote-getting organizations based on mass clientelism. At least so far, these traditional practices have worked well in the modern context. Who is to say that they or other traditional values and practices will not prove equally adaptable to the needs of the postindustrial age? To the extent that such cultural differences, deriving from different historical heritages, continue to distinguish one society from another, postindustrial politics in Japan will remain quite different from those in either the United States or Western Europe, in spite of the similarity or even identity of their stages of economic development and their common features as free societies.

Finally, political change in Japan has been retarded by the continuation of the LDP in power since 1955. Were it to lose its majority in the Diet, a completely new epoch in Japanese politics would suddenly open, possibly releasing economic and social energies now pent up and causing chain reactions in the political sphere. However this might speed up political change, the overwhelming majority of Japanese opinion leaders believe—as do I—that Japan is very unlikely to abandon its democratic institutions or negate its democratic values.

Part II
Political Participation Patterns

Chapter 4
Social Structure and Political Participation

Among American and Japanese specialists on Japanese politics, it is a well-known and long-established fact that political participation, not only in terms of voting but also in terms of group affiliation and other indicators, is higher in rural than in urban areas.[1] Japanese scholars and Japan specialists, however, have done very little so far to compare Japanese political participation with that of other societies and to draw implications for a general theory. And Western, especially American, political scientists who are not specialists on Japan have neglected the Japanese experience in their efforts to codify data on participation and construct theory. The neglect is understandable because both the language barrier and differences in research designs have, as a practical matter, made comparable data unavailable.

In explaining political participation in Japan, Japanese researchers and Japan scholars frequently advance the following propositions:

1. Political participation is higher in rural than in urban areas. High participation in rural areas is the result of social pressures or social norms which emphasize the value of participation *per se*.[2] Thus, political participation in rural areas is not a reflection of high political interest.[3]

[1]For rural-urban differences in voter turnout, see Kyōgoku and Ike (1959). Concerning group affiliation, politicians are recruiting larger numbers for their "personal support groups" from rural areas (see Langdon, 1967; Thayer, 1969; Curtis, 1971). For a description of various social groups in hamlets, see Fukutake (1967).

[2]Langdon (1967, pp. 89–90) likes to mention "group emphasis" as one of the main characteristics of the Japanese political culture which heavily affects political participation.

[3]The argument on this point is usually more sophisticated: If by political interest we mean sensitivity to the personal advantage that politics can bring, then political

2. Urban residents are generally better educated and have higher-level occupations than rural residents. This leads to greater political interest among them than among rural residents. However, the high level of political interest among urban residents is not related to political participation, because of the disintegration of a sense of community in cities, the failure of people to join associations, and the spread of a sense of futility.[4]

3. The mode of political participation in Japan is, thus, characterized by a high degree of mobilization in rural areas (high participation with little political interest) and a high degree of alienation in urban areas (low participation with high political interest) (Flanigan, 1968, p. 13). Despite the phenomenal economic prosperity and seeming political stability in recent years, democracy in Japan is still troubled by contradictions and strains, as revealed in its participation structure.

In contrast to the above propositions made by Japanese researchers, American political scientists formulate propositions of a very general sort. For example, Norman Nie and his associates (1969, p. 808) have suggested the following:

> Economic development alters the social structure of a nation. As nations become more economically developed, three major changes occur: (1) the relative size of the upper and middle classes becomes greater; (2) larger numbers of citizens are concentrated in the urban areas; and (3) the density and complexity of economic and secondary organizations increases. These social changes imply political changes. Greater proportions of the population find themselves in life situations which lead to increased political information, political awareness, sense of personal political efficacy, and other relevant attitudes. These attitude changes, in turn, lead to increases in political participation.

Recently, several comparative surveys have been conducted, and there has been an effort to standardize the data.[5] The "Cross-

interest is fairly widespread in Japan. However, if by political interest we mean concern for problems remote from a public viewpoint, then rural people give little evidence of having it (Watanuki, 1966).

[4]These sorts of propositions were frequently advanced around 1957–59 about the development of "mass society" in Japan.

[5]R. E. Ward and A. Kubota conducted a nationwide survey on Japanese electoral

Table 4.1: Pearson correlation coefficients

	SEX	RURURBN	SESIND3	NATEFF	POLINFO	INTEREST
SEX						
RURURBN	.059					
SESIND3	−.251	.122				
NATEFF	−.037	−.001	.015			
POLINFO	−.188	.041	.253	.052		
INTEREST	−.267	−.021	.237	.169	.238	
PARTICIP	−.279	−.193	.133	.159	.165	.454

SEX = Male 1, Female 2
RURURBN = Rural 1, Urban 2, Metropolitan 3
SESIND3 = SESIND collapsed into three equal categories, (low) 1, 2, 3 (high)
SESIND (Socioeconomic status of individual)
 = (INCOME−2.925)/1.548 + (MATERIAL−1.563)/1.117 + (EDFAM−2.782)/
 1.652 + (OCLEVRES−3.412)/1.629 (The minus figures are the means and the denominators are the standard deviations.)

MATERIAL (possession of refrigerator/car/credit card/telephone)
EDFAM (educational level of household head)
OCLEVRES (occupational level of respondents)
NATEFF (whether occupying positions affecting governmental behavior) = None 1, Some 2, Great Deal 3
POLINFO (Guttman scale of political knowledge questions) = (low) 1, 2, 3 (high)
INTEREST (level of political interest and discussion) = DISCNAT + LOCDISC + NATINRST = (low) 0, 1, 2, 3 (high)
PARTICIP (Participation scale) = NATVOTE + ELECTORAL (= NRALLY + POLORG) + ORGANIZE (= LOCWORK + FORMORG + NACTSOLV) + CONTACT (= EXCONT + COMELITI) = (low) 0, 1, 2, 3, 4, 5, 6, 7, 8, 9, 10 (high)

DISCNAT (frequency of discussion on national politics)
LOCDISC (frequency of discussion on local problems)
NATINRST (interest in national politics)
NATVOTE (participation in national elections)
NRALLY (frequency of attendance at political rallies)
POLORG = POLMEN + POLACT
POLMEN (number of affiliated political organizations)
POLACT (whether one is active in his affiliated organizations)
LOCWORK (whether working in solution of local problems)
FORMORG (participation in formation of local organizations)
NACTSOLV (number of problem-solving organizations in which one is active)
EXCONT (frequency of contact with elites above the local level)
COMELITI (first type of contacted political elite)

behavior and political socialization in 1967, and a number of young American scholars, such as Joseph A. Massey and James W. White, have been conducting surveys in Japan. The design of these surveys anticipates comparison with the data and propositions accumulated and codified mainly by American scholars. In this sense, they are comparative and standardized.

Table 4.2: Path coefficients

	X7 PARTICIP	X6 INTEREST	X5 POLIFO	X4 NATEFF	X3 SESIND 3	X2 RURURBN	X1 SEX
X6 INTEREST	.382	.382	.151	.157	.151	−.035	−.191
X5 POLINFO	.039	.057	.096	.043	.216	.022	−.133
X4 NATEFF	.087	.059	.004	.150	.006	−.000	−.036
X3 SESIND 3	.012	.057	.020	.001	.090	(.122)	(−.250)
X2 RURURBN	−.178	−.013	.002	.000	(.122)	−.189	(.059)
X1 SEX	−.157	−.073	−.012	−.005	(−.250)	(.591)	−.247
Total correlation		.454	.165	.159	.133	−.193	−.279
Direct effect		.382	.039	.087	.012	−.178	−.157
Indirect effect		—	.057	.063	.078	−.011	−.090
Total effect		.382	.096	.150	.090	−.189	−.247
Explained effect		.072	.068	.009	.043	−.003	−.032

Priority of variables: X1, X2 and X3 > X4 > X5 > X6
Ultimate dependent variable: X7
Exogenous variables: X1, X2 and X3
(The correlation between X1, X2 and X3 is not causally interpreted.)
Notes: 1) The numbers in the first column in the upper half of the table indicate the path coefficients between all the independent variables in the system and the final dependent variable—PARTICIP.
2) The numbers to the left of the main diagonal refer to the "mediated" effect by the variables listed on the top for the relationship between the final dependent variable and the independent variables listed at the left.
3) Numbers in the main diagonal boxes are the total causal effect of the variable listed on the top for the final dependent variable.
4) Numbers above the main diagonal are path coefficients of the reduced system.
5) "Explained effect" means the effect explained by the preceding variables, i.e. the amount of non-causal, spurious relationship between that particular variable and the ultimate dependent variable.
The format of presentation and the logic of interpretation used here are based on Kim (1969).

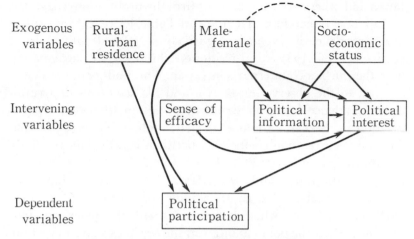

Fig. 4.1.   Seven-variable causal model

Notes: 1) Arrows between variables indicate path coefficients greater than 0.114 (three times the average standard error—0.038).
2) The almost isolated position of the "sense of efficacy" variable contrasts with the results of similar analyses relating to other countries. One possible reason for this is the inadequacy of the measure used in this analysis. Instead of the usual efficacy scale, only one question was used, asking whether the respondent thinks that he is in a position to influence governmental decisions.

National Research Program in Social and Political Change" (CPSPC)[6] is a large project to gather and analyze comparable data in quite heterogeneous societies India, Japan, Nigeria, and the United States. The surveys were conducted in 1966–67, and the analysis is still going on. Utilizing the CPSPC Japanese data, I shall examine the propositions about political participation. More specifically, I shall test the causal influence of six variables— urban-rural residence (RURURBN), sex (SEX), socioeconomic status of the individual (SESIND3), sense of efficacy (NATEFF), political information (POLINFO), and political interest (IN-TEREST)—on political participation (PARTICIP) in Japan.

The results of analysis show an amazing difference between

[6]The main participants in the Cross-National Research Program in Social and Political Change were Sidney Verba (U.S.A.), Ikeuchi Hajime (Japan), Rajini Kothari (India), and Ulf Himmelstrand (Sweden). Publications resulting from the project are: Verba, Ahmed, and Bhatt (1971), Verba, Nie, and Kim (1971), Verba and Nie (1972), Ikeuchi (1974), Verba, Nie, and Kim (forthcoming).

Japan and other countries, and confirm the propositions suggested by Japanese researchers. The data in Table 4.1 reveal that rural-urban residence in Japan is negatively correlated with political participation (–.193): rural residents exhibit higher participation than their urban counterparts in Japan. This finding offers a clear contrast to the observation of Nie and his associates that rural-urban residence bears no significant relation to political participation in the five nations that they studied. They report that the simple correlation coefficients between rural-urban residence and participation are: .068 (U.S.), –.023 (U.K.), –.022 (Germany), –.002 (Italy), and .073 (Mexico). Moreover, in Japan the level of political interest shows a high correlation with political participation (.454), which is consistent with the general pattern that the greater the political interest, the greater the participation.

The results of path analysis of Japanese participation data are reported in Table 4.2 and Fig. 4.1. Rural-urban residence has a fairly strong and direct effect on political participation (total effect is –.189, of which the direct effect is –.178). Of all the variables, political interest has the highest direct effect on participation (.382). Socioeconomic status and sex affect political interest fairly strongly (.151 and –.191 respectively), but rural-urban residence does not (–.035).

Thus rural residence (a term which connotes not only the physical surroundings but also the social structure and norms of rural villages) directly increases political participation. However, the "mobilization" proposition is not necessarily proved. In terms of levels of political information and interest, there is not much difference between rural and urban residents, so we cannot say that rural people are less informed and less interested. In contrast, the "alienation" proposition is definitely not borne out, for high political interest clearly correlates with high political participation. Socioeconomic status correlates positively with interest—the higher the status, the greater the interest; thus the universal development pattern manifests itself in Japan, too. Sex correlates more strongly, not because of the physiological difference but because of the social structures and norms associated with the male-female roles.

It is impossible to make a precise comparison with the analysis made by Nie and his associates since the casual models used are

different. In my model, the "organizational involvement" variable was not included, for two reasons. First, as I stated before,
my main intention was to test the propositions presented by Japanese scholars. Second, some technical difficulties stood in the way
of including some of the organizational involvement indices in
my causal model of political participation. Since a political participation index usually contains, as it does in this case, some
measure of involvement in political organization, we need special
indices of organizational involvement in order to avoid auto-
correlation. However, looking at the correlation between rural-
urban residence and organizational involvement in general ("in
general" including political organizations), we notice that the

Table 4.3:   Eighteen subgroups and participation
             Controlling:

Number of cases	SEX, SESIND3		SEX, RURURBN		RURURBN, SESIND3	
	Testing:					
	RURURBN		SESIND3		SEX	
109	RML	37.6%	RML	37.6%	RML	37.6%
100	UML	31.2	RMM	32.8	RFL	3.9
36	MML	11.1	RMH	45.0	RMM	32.8
124	RMM	32.8	RFL	3.9	RFM	15.2
174	UMM	24.3	RFM	15.2	RMH	45.0
60	MMM	13.8	RFH	20.0	RFH	20.0
117	RMH	45.0	UML	31.2	UML	31.2
233	UMH	39.4	UMM	24.3	UFL	6.4
122	MMH	12.4	UMH	39.4	UMM	24.3
140	RFL	3.9	UFL	6.4	UFM	15.5
227	UFL	6.4	UFM	15.5	UMH	39.4
74	MFL	2.9	UFH	11.5	UFH	20.0
76	RFM	15.2	MML	11.1	MML	11.1
183	UFM	15.5	MMM	13.8	MFL	2.9
67	MFM	9.6	MMH	12.4	MMM	13.8
43	RFH	20.0	MFL	2.9	MFL	2.9
120	UFH	11.5	MFM	9.6	MMH	12.4
56	MFH	13.8	MFH	13.8	MFH	13.8

Notes: 1) In the three-letter designation of subgroups, the first letter stands for
        Rural-Urban-Metropolitan; the second for Male-Female; and the third
        for Low-Middle-High socioeconomic status (SESIND3). For example,
        RML means Rural-Male-Low (*i.e.*, low in socioeconomic status).
        2) The percentages are of respondents in each sub-group who scored over 5
        on the participation scale (PARTICIP), *i.e.*, who were high in participa-
        tion.

correlation is the reverse of the usual pattern; *i.e.*, rural residence correlates with higher organizational involvement.

Considering the risk of applying to survey data—especially to such a qualitative dichotomous category as sex—a path analysis that assumes interval scales, I also tried to use traditional sub-group analysis. I broke down the sample into subgroups according to three independent variables—sex, rural-urban residence, and socioeconomic status—and obtained eighteen subgroups; I then examined the relationships between each of those independent variables and political participation. The results of this analysis are almost completely congruent with that of path analysis, except for several cases of "specification," which are shown by boxes in Table 4.3. That is, rural-urban residence, sex, and socioeconomic status are all independently related to the level of participation. The cases of "specification" suggest the following comments: (1) In the cases of RFL-UFL-MFL, the F and L factors are shown to play the decisive role in lowering the level of participation. (2) In the cases of UML-UMM-UMH and MML-MMM-MMH, socioeconomic status is shown to have nothing to do with the level of participation on the part of urban and metropolitan males, thus lending some support to the proposition concerning "alienation" (prevalence of high political interest and low political participation). In other words, the subgroups UMM, UMH, MMM, and MMH tend to be high in political interest and low in participation (see Table 4.4). (3) In the related cases of MMH-MFH, male-female differences disappear as a result of a lower level of participation among MMH and a higher level of participation among MFH. The level of political information increases in the second of these subgroups (MFH), permitting the generalization that in a metropolitan environment a rise in socioeconomic status can bring an increase in political knowledge and consequently an increase in political participation.

Table 4.4 shows variations in various measures of participation and interest among eighteen subgroups. One can see a perfectly consistent pattern among the measures which were used to construct the participation scale (NATVOTE and NRALLY are examples). Rural-urban residence, sex, and socioeconomic status are all related to those measures. Moreover, as is to be expected

Table 4.4: Eighteen subgroups and measures of participation, interest, and information

Variables:	NATVOTE	NRALLY	DISCNAT	INTEREST	POLINFO
Values:	Always voted	Four or more	More than once a week	High (3.00)	High (3.00)
RML	84.7%	50.5%	46.7%	27.4%	36.3%
UML	69.3	39.0	42.1	23.5	34.3
MML	61.1	22.2	40.0	19.4	30.6
RMM	81.5	43.5	55.0	19.4	39.5
UMM	76.3	47.1	52.6	21.9	42.1
MMM	72.9	35.0	64.0	28.3	55.0
RMH	93.0	39.0	77.9	48.7	59.0
UMH	79.2	45.5	70.4	36.3	54.7
MMH	69.7	25.4	71.4	28.5	51.2
RFL	76.3	17.1	23.4	9.0	15.9
UFL	69.6	21.1	33.6	6.4	18.4
MFL	58.9	6.8	35.8	7.9	21.1
RFM	77.3	28.9	35.6	10.5	27.6
UFM	75.6	21.1	41.9	15.7	36.2
MFM	52.9	16.4	45.6	13.0	29.0
RFH	85.0	27.9	56.4	20.9	32.6
UFH	66.4	25.8	53.2	21.3	40.2
MFH	70.4	14.3	68.0	14.3	42.9

on the basis of previous analyses, socioeconomic status and sex have a clear and significant relationship with political interest and political information. Further, we can clarify somewhat the relationship between political interest and political information, on the one hand, and the urban-rural variable, on the other. Male and female subgroups show opposite patterns of relationships with respect to DISCNAT (frequency of discussion on national politics) and POLINFO (amount of political information) depending on rural-urban residence. Male rural residents score higher in these measures than male urban and metropolitan residents, whereas female rural residents score lower. In other words, rural females are higher in participation and urban females are higher in interest and information. This raises the question of whether, in terms of the propositions given earlier concerning alienation (high political interest and low participation) and mobilization (low political interest and high participation), we can say that the urban female scores high on alienation and that the rural female scores high on mobilization. Taking into account such facts as the increased tendency of urban females to vote,[7] I would like to interpret it as a sign of increasing political interest on their part and would like to predict a rise in levels of participation by urban females in the future. That is, I would like to interpret it as a kind of time-lag phenomenon where change that has already occurred in some respects will cause other changes later.[8]

This analysis has revealed the existence of certain patterns of relationships in Japan between different variables and political participation. Some of them are also found in other countries— e.g., the relationships that appear among sex, socioeconomic status, political interest, and political participation. But one of the patterns revealed by this analysis calls for special attention from the comparative point of view: the existence in Japan of a reverse relationship between rural-urban residence and political partic- ipation. (In rural areas, participation is higher not only in terms of voting but also in terms of a synthesized participation scale.)

Why is this the case, and what are the implications for the pursuit of a general theory of political participation? The follow- ing appear to be among the reasons for the peculiar Japanese pattern:

1. The long-established, historical social structure of the vil- lage, which still survives, communal in character, with a high density of social relationships, nourishing norms and exerting pressures for conformity in various areas of behavior, in which voting and other kinds of political participation have come to be included. One can argue against this immediately. A village social structure with a high density of social relationships and a com- munal character is not limited to Japan. It exists also in Korea and other Asian societies, especially where rice growing in paddy fields is dominant. To be sure, a high voter turnout in rural areas is reported in Korea's case also, but in regard to other measures, except for membership in political parties, participation in the

----

[7]Ever since 1946, when suffrage was extended to women, voter turnout has been lower among females than among males. However, the difference has been decreasing. In recent elections in cities, voter turnout has been consistently higher among females than among males. This reversal has not occurred in towns and villages, and probably never will.

[8]See the "arrow scheme" in Lazarsfeld, Barton, and Lipset (1954).

rural areas of Korea is reported to be lower than in the urban areas (Lee, 1969, 1971).

2. The politicization of the periphery (Rokkan, 1970) through the gradual extension of suffrage since 1890 and through the use of neighborhood associations congruent with the village social structure. Beginning in 1890, when only 1.13 percent of the total population was qualified to vote,[9] suffrage was extended successively in 1902, 1920, 1928, and 1946; by 1928 all males over 25 could vote, and in 1946 universal male and female suffrage was introduced. The gradual process involved the smooth politicization of successive groups and brought a continuously high voter turnout. Needless to say, Japan differs from the other new states of Asia in terms of the gradual entry of the periphery into politics. Further, as specialists on Japan often point out, ever since the nation-building of the Meiji era, the government has tried to maintain the solidarity of the village community insofar as this could be done consistently with the pursuit of other goals, such as the promotion of an efficient and viable administrative system. (Fukutake, 1967; Steiner, 1968). Neighborhood associations were formed (whether or not sponsored by the government), and membership in them was encouraged or enforced, especially during the totalitarian mobilization of 1937 to 1945. The legacy persists in the prevalence of neighborhood associations in contemporary Japan.

3. The spread of education concomitant with or preceding the extension of suffrage. This factor is an important addition to the other two. After the promulgation of a decree on education in 1872, compulsory education was actually introduced in 1879; it was extended to four years in 1886, to six years in 1908, and finally to nine years in 1947. The spread of education has made it possible to maintain a high voter turnout from the beginning, even though the voter is required to handwrite the name of the candidate on the voting slip.

The implications of the above for a general theory of political participation are not entirely clear. Certainly we can argue that if the three factors that coexisted and mutually reinforced one another in Japan should appear in the same form in some other

---

[9]Taking into account elections for local assemblies, the date goes back to 1878.

country, the possibility would be high that a similar pattern of participation would occur. However, the second and third factors are historically peculiar to Japan, and in this age of universal suffrage it is too late for them to appear in other countries. So the question concerns the extent of the influence of the first factor—a village social structure, communal in character, with a high density of social relationships. As is shown in Korea's case, a high voter turnout and affiliation with political parties can occur if voting and affiliation with political parties are associated with village norms and pressures that demand conformity. Moreover, in a village environment, associations often take on a communal character. In principle, they might be used outside Japan to promote political participation—a possibility that raises the question of what the functions or dysfunctions would be of this kind of a fusion of deliberately established associations and already existing communal structures and norms.[10]

[10]As Satish K. Arora has pointed out, the other side of this problem is the degree of integration of alienation among urban residents in developing societies: "We find that not merely is there the possibility that urban residents will be less likely than rural ones to participate in political activity; but effects of urbanization may make long-term residents even more prone to a kind of alienation which, even in comparison with short-term residents, make them less likely to participate in any conventional activity, and more prone to nonconventional protesting and rioting" (Arora, 1971). See also Nelson (1970). This raises the question of the significance of nonconventional modes of political participation and calls attention to the importance of political skills to absorb them.

Chapter 5
Tradition and Modernity in Voting Behavior in the 1950s

This chapter will attempt to interpret the pattern of politics in present-day Japan, paying special attention to the political allegiance of the white-collar group. Political characteristics for this group show certain tendencies peculiar to modern Japan, and which might aid in the understanding of the more general pattern of politics. In the interpretation, I have tried to introduce multicontextual considerations as much as possible. Although this chapter is essentially a monocontextual study, by introducing such multicontextual considerations,[1] we can expect a more sophisticated interpretation concerning the pattern of politics in this particular case, and we can contribute to knowledge of other societies which are relatively highly industrialized but still moving and changing under the impact of the industrialization process.

What is the meaning of "multicontextual" considerations? In terms of stages of industrialization, Japan passed the initial stages long ago; now it may be compared in many ways with present-day Italy or France. But it is an industrialized society in what is called the non–Western world, and this uniqueness has meaning beyond geographical location. Lucian Pye (1958) has tried to present an analytical scheme for understanding a non–Western political process; he presents seventeen characteristics of such a process. Although Japan is not non–Western in the sense of being in the process of passing from traditional society to industrialization, we find that eight characteristics out of the seventeen which

---

[1]That is, this chapter is intended to be a monocontextual study which contains some elements of multicontextual study. I intend also to go beyond mere description of patterns and to inquire into causal factors. In this sense, this chapter is meant to be comparative.

Pye enumerated still persist in present-day Japan to a considerable degree but for different reasons than Pye suggested.[2] Although this article will not deal historically with problems of initial industrialization and its political consequence in Japan, it will pay attention to certain limiting factors still working in current Japanese politics which arose from Japan's position as a latecomer in the race to industrialize and as a member of the non–Western world.

Voting Behavior: The Patterns

The pattern of voting behavior in modern Japan[3] points up four characteristics different from the general tendencies usually found in Western European societies.[4]

First, if we classify political parties on a continuum of left-right,[5] usually there is demonstrated a tendency for low-income groups to vote for leftist parties (Lipset, 1960, ch. 7). In the case of Japan, however, on the basis of nationwide poll data, it is difficult to recognize clearly any relationship between income group and party choice. If there is any, the relationship seems to be very weak.[6]

[2]The characteristics among the seventeen Pye enumerated which might be found in present-day Japan are: "1. The political sphere is not sharply differentiated from the sphere of social and personal relations. 2. Political parties tend to take on a world view and represent a way of life. 4. The character of political loyalty gives political leaders a high degree of freedom in determining politics. 8. There are sharp differences in the political orientation of the generations. 9. Little consensus exists as to the legitimate ends and means of political action. 11. Roles are highly interchangeable. 15. The affective or expressive aspect of politics tends to override the problem-solving or public-policy aspect." In a later book, Pye chose the word "transitional" rather than "non–Western" to describe these characteristics.

[3]In Japan, official election statistics do not give us information about the various sociological characteristics of the voters. The data used in the analysis in this chapter are drawn mainly from various public opinion polls.

[4]We can add one more characteristic which concerns the voting rate. Usually in Western societies, the voting rate in cities is higher than that in rural districts. In Japan, the voting rate is higher in rural districts than in cities. The reason for this is that in rural districts the pressure to vote is great because of strong village solidarity and the idea that voting is an obligation to the community. (See Chapter 4.)

[5]In Japan, this continuum would include: on the extreme left, the Japan Communist Party, then the Japan Socialist Party as left-wing socialists, then the Democratic Socialist Party as right-wing socialists; on the right, the Liberal Democratic Party as a coalition of various conservative factions. The extreme rightist parties are split and their votes are negligible.

[6]Data concerning correlation between income level and party choice is usually

Table 5.1: Party choice among occupational groups, November 1960
(in percentages)

	LDP	JSP	DSP	Miscellaneous	Non-partisan	D. K.	Non-voter
Farmers and fishermen	70.1	17.5	3.6	0.3	0.3	1.4	6.8
Merchants and small manufacturers	64.8	19.6	4.0	0.6	1.2	—	9.7
White-collar	31.8	44.0	4.9	1.5	0.4	0.4	17.0
Manual workers	31.0	43.2	1.1	2.7	2.1	5.2	14.7
Housewives	51.2	25.2	5.4	0.3	0.6	3.2	14.0

Source: Answers to the question, "For which party did you vote in the election of the members of the House of Representatives in 1960?" gathered by a nationwide sample survey conducted by Shimbun Yoronchōsa Renmei (Public Opinion Survey League for the Presses) just after the election.

Note: In this sort of public opinion survey, the ratio of people who answer that they voted for the Communist Party is usually 1 percent or less (the actual vote for the Communist Party is usually 3 percent of the total votes). Perhaps this research agency included the answers for the Communist Party into the category of "Miscellaneous" because of the small number of such answers.

Second, with regard to party choice of certain occupational groups, the high rate of support for leftist parties (predominantly for the Japan Socialist Party) among the white-collar group is striking. As shown in Table 5.1, in the white-collar group, support for the Socialists exceeds that for the Liberal Democratic Party. The Japan Socialist Party, in terms of its ideology and rhetoric at least, can be regarded as a left-wing socialist party, whose counterpart we cannot find in Western European societies (except perhaps the Socialist Party in Italy). Although it is not statistically significant in the table, if we add the support for the Democratic Socialists to that for the Socialists, support for these two parties among the white-collar group is greater than support among manual workers. Although the intellectuals' inclination to be more radical, to support the (relative) Left more than the other strata, is a rather universal phenomenon in Western societies, it should be noted that the white-collar group in Western societies supports the

omitted from the publications of opinion survey data. For available published data, see Nihon Shakaigakka· Chōsa-iinkai (1958, p. 308).

right-wing socialists to a considerable degree, along with some support for the conservatives or the liberals. The high rate of support for the socialists, especially for the left socialists, among the Japanese white-collar group as a whole is not paralleled in any Western European society.

A third correlation in the analysis of voting behavior is made in terms of educational level. In most industrialized societies, the higher the level of education, the higher the voting rate. But correlation between educational levels and party choice remains vague in most Western societies. In the case of Japan, there is a fairly clear correlation between educational level and party choice —the better educated tend to support the Left (Table 5.2).[7]

Table 5.2:   Party choice and educational level, November 1960
               (in percentages)

	LDP	JSP	DSP	Miscellaneous	Non-partisan candidates	D. K.	Non-voter
Low educational level[a]	57.0	22.2	4.0	0.6	0.4	1.9	13.9
Medium educational level[b]	46.2	34.8	5.0	0.7	0.9	0.7	11.6
High educational level[c]	39.2	35.0	7.7	—	2.1	—	16.1

Source: Same as Table 5.1.

[a]Low educational level: those who finished sixth or eighth grade elementary-school work (before World War II) and those who finished ninth grade junior-high-school work (after World War II).

[b]Medium educational level: those who were graduated from eleventh grade middle school (before World War II) or twelfth grade senior high school (after World War II).

[c]High educational level: those who graduated from various forms of higher educational institutions (before World War II) or universities and colleges (after World War II).

[7] In this connection, it may be argued that, since the chances for higher education have expanded since World War II owing to education-reform programs, those who are in the "high educational level" bracket will largely be members of the younger generation; their party choice thus might be more heavily influenced by the age factor than by the education factor. However, contrary to the belief that after World War II Japan established a tremendous number of universities and colleges at a single stroke, the fact is that higher educational institutions had already developed before and during the war. Therefore, the age distribution of those with high educational levels is not necessarily so skewed in the direction of the younger generation. What did expand amazingly after World War II was middle-level education (the senior high school system). Consequently, the age distribution of those having completed middle-level education is heavily concentrated in the twenties, and we certainly can see the influence of the age factor in the party choices of this group.

Fourth, the universal tendency for younger groups to support the Left and older groups to show a more conservative inclination (Lipset, 1960, ch. 8) is clearly illustrated in Japan's case. As shown in Table 5.3, there are three political generations in Japan.

Table 5.3:   Party choice and age groups, November 1960 (in percentages)

Age	LDP	JSP	DSP	Miscel-laneous	Non-partisan candi-dates	D. K.	Non-voter
20–29	37.6	37.1	5.1	1.2	0.3	0.5	18.1
30–39	50.1	32.2	4.9	0.4	0.3	0.7	11.3
40–49	59.4	23.0	5.1	0.2	1.0	2.0	9.4
Over 50	62.8	15.0	3.7	0.5	0.9	2.6	14.5

Source: Same as Tables 5.1 and 5.2

Those in their twenties (born between 1930 and 1940) and educated after World War II show a high rate of support for the Socialists.[8] Those in their thirties and forties tend to vote for middle-of-the-road parties. Those in their fifties and older are distinctly conservative. Incidentally, the size of the 20–29 group is roughly equal to the group over 50. Thus the radical 20–29 group and the conservative over 50 group balance out around the middle-of-the-road 30–49 group.

Voting Behavior: Some Explanations

How can we properly explain these four characteristics of voting behavior by various groups in present-day Japanese society?

The lack of clear correlation between income groups and party choice can be explained in terms of two factors. The first factor is technical: It is difficult to evaluate the income of Japanese farmers accurately by usual questionnaire-type survey techniques, because a considerable part of what otherwise would be their household

[8] Whether this group will retain their inclination to support the Left in their old age remains to be seen. There will be a number of defections as they climb the social ladder and take on more mature roles. But it is also probable that the life style of this generation will remain radically different from that of other generations. Whether the Conservatives can absorb large numbers from this generation depends on various factors, such as whether the party can modernize.

expenses is covered by the crops they raise. Therefore, because opinion polls cannot allocate much time or space to subtle distinctions, many farmers are included in the low-income group even though their actual income might be quite high. As stated before, farmers predominantly are supporters of the Liberal Democratic Party. This naturally makes the correlation between income level and party choice ambiguous.

However, apart from such a technical problem, it is still true that the Liberal Democrats command the majority of support among lower strata in rural villages and also substantial support among urban lower strata. In rural villages, the reasons for this support are the economic structure of agriculture and the social structure of the village in Japan. Japanese agriculture is predominantly based on small owner-cultivators. Even the poorest Japanese farmers are small farmers cultivating their own land with family labor. In this respect, the political situation in the rural sector of Japan is quite different from that of Italy, where vast numbers of tenant farmers and agricultural workers are organized by leftists, mainly communists. Even in France and Sweden, where small farming is the dominant form, considerable numbers of agricultural workers are employed, and many of them are supporters of the socialists.[9] The conservativeness of this kind of peasantry has been repeatedly pointed out by various writers. In addition, the social structure of the Japanese rural village offers the opportunity for the dominance of conservative values. Need for cooperation in the control of water for irrigation, common worship of village Shinto gods, common ties to the same Buddhist temple, concentrated physical location of houses in a narrow area, networks of extended family ties and other conjugal ties, and the administrative practice of utilizing the village as an administrative unit (a practice long established and maintained from the feudal past through the process of modernization in the Meiji era, 1868–1911)—these conditions had created a high degree of village solidarity and (especially before land reform after World War II)

[9]According to labor statistics, in Japan the number of males employed in agriculture and forestry in 1962 was 370,000; a considerable part of this figure represents forestry workers. In contrast, in Italy, the number of male agricultural workers in 1962 was 1,200,000 (Instituto Centrale di Statistica, *Bollettino Mensile di Statistica*, August 1963). Most of these workers were organized under CGIL (see La Palombara, 1957). For France, see Laponce (1961). With regard to Sweden, see Rustow (1956, p. 181).

hierarchical interpersonal relationships (Fukutake, 1962). The Conservatives have taken advantage of this solidarity and pattern of hierarchy which, although shaken by land reform, still remains, especially in mountainous villages where landlords who own and run the forests still dominate village affairs. In such areas, support for the Conservatives has solidified, and infiltration by the leftists has been thwarted. The poorer the farmer, the more he is vulnerable to the political values in the village and to pressure from powerful people who have good reasons for being conservative.[10]

In cities, we see a fairly clear correlation between income level and party choice, *i.e.*, the lower the income level, the more support for the Socialists. But as Table 5.4 shows, the Conservatives are getting fairly strong support among people in the lowest income bracket.[11] This phenomenon is neither strange nor peculiar to present-day Japan. A similar tendency is reported in Sweden (Rustow, 1955, p. 141); and in Japan's case, those in the lowest income group live in an environment where traditional values are prevalent, so that it is no wonder that they show an inclination to support the Conservatives.

Recently a Buddhist sect called Sōka Gakkai (Value Creation Society) gathered its followers and, in local elections and the election for the House of Councillors, ran its own candidates. They received four million votes. According to available survey data,

---

[10]To keep peace within itself and to act as a unit are two of the important political norms of the village community. This is what Lucian Pye (1958) called the "communal basis of politics." After World War II, just before land reform was instituted, farmers' unions or leagues were rapidly organized. In order to keep peace in the villages, often all farmers in each village—including landlords and part-time farmers who engaged in farming only on Sundays and holidays—would join the village's union or league. These groups rapidly lost their strength after land reform.

In local elections, the village community usually recommends the candidate for whom all the villagers are expected to vote. In extreme cases where the campaigning is intense and the vote is close, watchers are posted on the roads at the entrance to the village in order to block infiltration by the candidates of other villages. We should not overlook the role of traditional values here. The lower the social stratum, the less educated are its members and the more tightly they hold traditional values: subservience to superiors, conformity to village norms, and so on. These values internally motivate people to vote for the Conservatives, even when pressures from outside are weak or nonexistent.

[11]Again, a technical problem should be noted. In Japan, where age is one of the main factors determining wages, younger people are included in the low-income brackets in disproportionate numbers. Considering this age factor, which reinforces the tendency to support the leftists, we can assume that poor older people are strongly inclined to the conservative view.

Table 5.4:   Party choice and income (in percentages)

Monthly income	Liberal Democrats	Socialists	Democratic Socialists	Other answers (including D. K.)
0	37	38	6	19
0–10	33	33	6	28
10–15	26	43	3	28
15–20	25	50	4	21
20–30	32	48	4	16
30–40	39	47	4	10
40–50	37	43	7	13
50–60	52	33	6	9
60–80	49	29	6	16
80–100	69	12	9	10
Over 100	79	8	5	8

Source: A survey conducted by Minshushugi Kenkyūkai among samples of males over 20 living in Tokyo ward districts in February 1961.

Note:. The unit of monthly income is 1,000 yen (about U.S. $3.00).

this group is recruiting its followers mainly from the uneducated, lower-income group and among unskilled manual workers (but not exclusively—we can find intellectuals and high-income people such as an actress, a professional baseball pitcher, and the wife and daughter of a University of Tokyo professor among its followers, but these are small in number). The age composition of its followers is interesting: the Sōka Gakkai boasts the strength of youth organizations. Actually, according to survey data in a lower-class residential section of Tokyo,[12] about half of this group's followers are youths in their twenties. Two comments may be ventured: politically, half of these youths, who compose the followers of the Sōka Gakkai, are recruited from potential supporters of the leftists. The other half are drawn from potential supporters of the Conservatives. Hence, the effects of political activities of the Sōka Gakkai can work equally unfavorably to the leftists and the Conservatives. Second, the growth of Sōka Gakkai can be regarded as a sign of the partial collapse of traditional values. The Sōka Gakkai attacks, although vaguely, the corruption of the establishment, emphasizes the immediate benefits which can be

[12]A survey conducted by sociology students at the University of Tokyo in 1963.

Table 5.5:   Party choice among various strata of manual workers
(in percentages)

1. In Tokyo ward districts

	LDP	JSP	DSP	Others (D. K., no response)
Workers in large enterprises[a]	9	76	5	10
Workers in medium and small enterprises	20	57	4	19
Artisans	39	30	6	24
Workers without stable jobs	33	40	2	25

2. In a local city near Kobe (Miki city, population 38,000)

	LDP	JSP	DSP	JCP	Others (D. K., no response)
Workers in large enterprises[a]	21	46	19	—	14
Workers in medium enterprises[b]	47	35	11	—	6
Workers in small enterprises[c]	46	37	7	—	10

3. In an industrial city in northern Kyushu where the biggest steel mill in Japan is located (Yawata city, population 330,000).

	LDP	JSP	DSP	JCP	No votes	Others (D. K., no response)
Workers in large enterprises[a]	8	78	5	1	7	1
Workers in medium and small enterprises	22	57	2	4	14	1

Source: (1) A survey conducted by Minshushugi Kenkyūkai among samples of males over 20 years in Tokyo ward districts in February 1961. (2) A survey conducted by the author in February 1962. (3) A survey conducted by the author in December 1960.

[a]Those that employ over 500 employees.
[b]Those have 50–499 employees.
[c]Those that have 1–49 employees.

gained by believing in its values, and, within its hierarchy of positions, emphasizes the principle of achievement, which attracts especially those youths who have low educational achievement levels and cannot expect much promotion in their jobs. As S. M. Lipset (1958) put it, it is universal that,

> once the lowest strata are broken from their allegiance to traditional values and come to believe that a change for the better is possible, they tend to back a political tendency which offers an immediate and relatively uncomplex solution to their problem.

Let us now try to explain the comparatively high ratio of support for the leftists among white-collar workers in Japan. Why do Japanese manual workers support leftist parties only to the same extent as (or even to a lesser extent than) do white-collar workers? The manual worker group in Japan, although statistically regarded as homogeneous, is really highly heterogeneous. If we look at the manual worker group in terms of the size of enterprises where they work and the locality where they live, we are struck by the correlations with their party choice (see Table 5.5). Those who are employed in medium-size enterprises and especially in small family enterprises show a tendency similar to their employers —a tendency toward the old middle class in their party choice and also in their social attitudes. The majority of those workers are not organized in labor unions, and they are living in an environment where traditional values are prevalent. Although this sort of tendency in terms of party choice and social attitudes is rather universal (Lipset, 1960, p. 262–64), what is characteristic of Japan's case is the vast number of such "Tory" workers. According to the author's estimate, the Liberal Democrats are getting roughly five million votes from this group of manual workers and their families (see Fig. 5.1).[13] The voting behavior of "Tory" workers lowers the average ratio of workers' support for the leftist parties in the nationwide survey data. If we compare the party

[13]According to the statistics, in 1960, 54.8 percent of employees in all industries (excluding agriculture and fishing, domestic service, and other service industries) were working in enterprises with less than thirty employees. Such workers are under the strong influence of traditional values because of their living environment and the influence of their employers. The Political Organization for Medium and Small-size Enterprises (*Chūshōkigyō Seiji-renmei*) boasts that it represents over 12 million votes, including the votes of employers and employees and their families. But actually this organization has succeeded in organizing only a fraction of this group.

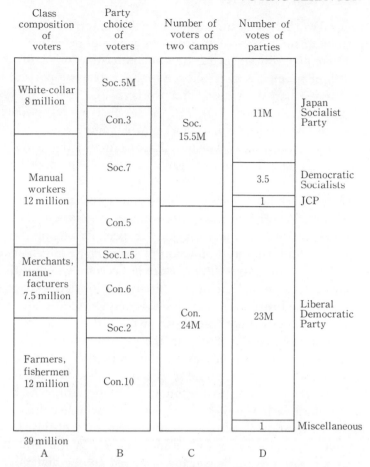

Fig. 5.1.   Japanese voters, 1960

Notes: This figures is based on the following assumptions and procedures:
1) Total electorate is about 54 million, 73 percent of whom voted in 1960; thus 39 million votes were cast.
2) To make the chart simple, we assume that female voters voted in the same way as their husbands or fathers. In Japan's case, this has been substantiated by opinion polls. This is different from the Italian case, where women strongly favor the Christian Democrats, regardless of male preference.
3) The voting rate of farmers, small merchants, and manufacturers is higher than that of white-collar and manual workers. The sizes of the classes of voters in column A are estimated by taking into consideration this different rate of voting and using the Census statistics on the occupational composition of male population gainfully engaged in economic activities.
4) In columns B and C, Communist and Democratic Socialist votes are combined with those of Socialists. Also, miscellaneous minor parties and independent candidates votes are included in Conservative.

choices of workers who are working in big enterprises or plants with those of the white-collar group as a whole, or with those of the white-collar contingent in the same enterprise or plant, then clearly those manual workers show a higher rate of support for the leftist parties than the white-collar workers do.

Still, we have a fairly high rate of support for leftist parties among Japanese white-collar workers, in comparison with the white-collar groups in all Western European societies. How can we explain it? This phenomenon is not caused by any single factor, but it is the result of the coincidence of many. First, the age factor might be at work here, because white-collar jobs have rapidly expanded since World War II, so the younger generation might be strongly represented in this category.[14] Especially among clerical workers, we find a large proportion of younger people. Lacking the available comparative data, we are not certain whether this is peculiar only to Japan, but since white-collar jobs are expanding rapidly in all industrialized societies, this may be a fairly universal phenomenon and will not sufficiently explain the tendency.

It is often pointed out that with the expansion of white-collar jobs, the economic status of white-collar workers tends to drop in comparison with that of manual workers; at the same time white-collar workers will cling to the image of high status which is a remnant of an earlier period. The question is whether this sort of relative deprivation is actually occurring in present-day Japan. Objectively speaking, a leveling of income after World War II in comparison with before the war has occurred among high government officials, top- and middle-management officials of big private enterprises, and professors at ex-imperial universities. Before World War II, these people had enjoyed relatively high incomes. But this cannot be regarded as the reason why ordinary white-collar workers support leftist parties today, because in the case of

[14]The following breakdown of occupational groups according to age (in percentages) was published by the Institute for Statistical Mathematics (1961, p. 472):

	20–29	30–39	40–49	50–59	60 +	
Professional and administrative	26	27	25	17	5	(N = 144)
Clerks	53	26	14	6	1	(N = 271)
Laborers	47	26	16	8	3	(N = 173)
Lower laborers	22	24	30	17	7	(N = 96)
Average	29	24	19	14	14	(N = 2,369)

ordinary white-collar workers, after the postwar recovery of the
economy, incomes did not drop below prewar levels. The subjective feeling of deprivation might be explained by the rising tide
of expectations after World War II. This rising tide of expectations affected not only white-collar workers but all strata; however, it may be argued that the impact of the rising tide of expectations would be strongest among white-collar workers because
they are more exposed to mass media and to urban living. Housing shortages, congestion in public transportation, high prices of
land for housing—these conditions undoubtedly contribute to the
discontent and the demand for more planning and intervention
by the government. But again these conditions affect all strata of
society.

Another factor influencing the voting behavior of white-collar
workers is the rapid and widespread unionization and subsequent
spread of egalitarian values among the white-collar group after
World War II. It is hard to tell what percentage of white-collar
workers are now organized, because in Japan labor unions were
organized on the basis of plant or enterprise and include both
manual and white-collar workers within one organization, except
in the case of mining industries. White-collar workers (because of
the union shop concept) automatically become members of the
labor union of each plant or enterprise if one exists. Even in an
enterprise where the majority of the employees are white-collar
(e.g., in banks, schools, and public offices), unions were organized
rapidly after World War II and maintained to the present. As a
matter of fact, public servants are one of the most highly unionized
groups (67.2 percent). Because of their mixed membership, because of their emergence just after World War II when destruction
and poverty made everyone equal, and because of their nature as
unions, labor unions have emphasized egalitarian values and solidarity (although often in practice this means solidarity as employees of the same enterprise). It has been pointed out that in the British and Swedish cases, white-collar unions tend to emphasize and
try to maintain the difference between their interests and those of
manual workers, in terms of interests such as wages, working
hours, vacations, promotions, and so forth. Politically they are
often led by "liberal" rather than socialist leaders. However, in
terms of their instrumental interests—legal recognition of labor

unions, the right to strike, and so on—they show solidarity with manual workers' unions (Lockwood, 1958, pp. 195–96; Galenson, 1961, p. 84). What is different in Japan is that, although white-collar workers feel a difference in status and certainly want to maintain and enlarge it whenever possible, this sort of demand has no legitimacy in Japanese labor unions, with their mixed membership and their ideology which emphasizes solidarity. This is not to say that Japanese white-collar workers conform completely to this egalitarian value and ideology. As a matter of fact, they do feel that they should be treated differently from manual workers and often are discontented because their mixed-membership union is dominated by such workers and does not represent their interests well; often the white-collar workers split the union in the case of prolonged and intensified strikes. What I wish to suggest is that, where labor unions emphasize egalitarian values, chances are greater that the white-collar group will behave solidly with manual workers, at least officially, and in doing so internalize the norm of solidarity to some degree. I also do not wish to suggest that membership in labor unions among white-collar employees guarantees their active participation in union activity. On the contrary, generally speaking, they are inactive members. There are, however, several militant unions which are composed mainly of white-collar members; also one can find active union members and leaders from the white-collar group in unions with mixed membership. In this context, I will introduce a fourth factor: resentment toward the status hierarchy among lower white-collar workers, especially those working in government bureaucracies.

In spite of post–World War II reforms, promotion to higher positions in government bureaucracies is open only to those who graduated from particular universities (mainly ex-imperial universities). Those graduates can expect rapid promotion and various fringe benefits attached to higher positions. Those who are excluded from this privileged route of promotion naturally feel discontentment toward such a system, and the younger they are, the more discontented they feel. Moreover, before World War II, until 1918, only the imperial universities had been legally *the* universities, and even after that there had existed two kinds of institutions of higher learning. One was the university and the other was the "higher institution for professional training," which required fewer years of study and therefore was more accessible to those from poorer families. These two had formed a legitimate hierarchy of schools and their graduates. After World War II, the educational reform standardized all institutions of higher learning, giving them the same legal status as the universities. However, in practice, differential treatment according to the particular universities concerned still definitely exists.[15] This fosters more discontent and resentment among those alienated from the privileged route than in pre–World War II days. In the Union for Taxation Stations' Personnel, the Union of Clerks in Judicial Administration, the Union of Agricultural Ministry Employees, and among clerks in postal service and in railways within the Postal Workers' Union and National Railway Union, this sort of resentment is the basis for members' support for militant union activities and ideologies. To some extent, this resentment and discontent can be suppressed and transformed into conformity with the status hierarchy: those who are alienated from the privileged route of promotion can expect some kind of lesser promotion by age seniority. To become active in militant union activity naturally jeopardizes one's position with respect to promotion, and many refrain from being marked as militant.

Those who are privileged (*i.e.*, those who are graduated from first-class universities), on the other hand, are not necessarily supporters of the Liberal Democrats. Often they become politically apathetic and do not vote. But when they vote, there are more who vote for the Socialists than for the Liberal Democrats (at least in the 30–39 group). Thus we find that a fifth factor at least hinders the white-collar workers from becoming ardent supporters of the Liberal Democrats: attitudes and values opposed to the traditionalism and anti-intellectualism of the Liberal Democrats. All opinion polls show a positive correlation between occupational group and attitude toward traditionalism. The white-collar group as a whole most strongly exhibits attitudes unfavorable to tradi-

[15]Individuals who graduate from evening colleges, while working in some government organization or private business during the day, have quite a precarious status. In most cases, they are not officially treated as college graduates. This causes discontentment among these individuals, who, in general, have more ability to learn and desire to climb the social ladder than many ordinary university students. In 1961, nearly 90,000 students were enrolled in evening colleges, making up about 12 percent of the total number of university students.

tional values (Matsumoto, 1960). Education has much to do with these attitudes. The better educated they are, the more these members are unfavorably disposed toward traditionalism. But this again is not peculiar to Japan. Generally speaking, higher education fosters rational and liberal thinking; Stouffer (1955) reported of United States society that the higher the educational level of a group, the more liberal and tolerant of political deviation it would be. We have seen that age can be correlated with attitudes toward traditionalism. The younger generation has an attitude unfavorable to traditional values in comparison with the older generation. In Japan this tendency is stronger than in other societies. And, particularly in Japan, these rational and liberal attitudes, which are unfavorable to traditionalism and to anti-intellectualism, are expressed as support for the leftist parties—mainly for the Socialists. To express this another way, it is an expression of distrust toward the Conservatives, *i.e.*, the Liberal Democrats. At the core of this problem is the nature of political alternatives in present-day Japan, a problem we will touch upon in the following section.

Japan's Cultural Politics

If we dare to characterize the basis of political alternatives in present-day Japan with a single concept, we might suggest "cultural politics" or "value politics."[16] By "cultural politics" I mean politics in which the cleavages caused by differences in value systems have more effect on the nature of political conflict than the cleavages caused by economic, or status, differences. This is not to deny the working of economic or status interests in Japanese politics, but rather to emphasize the relative dominance of cultural or value factors and the superimposition and effects of these factors on others.

As shown above, the governing conservative party—the Liberal Democratic Party—is recruiting its support mainly from older

---

[16] I have borrowed this concept from Hofstadter (1963, p. 82), who introduced it to supplement his previous concept of "status politics" in explaining the phenomenon of the rise of the radical Right in United States society. His intention in introducing this new concept seemed to be to correct the overemphasis on psychological factors due to status anxiety in the concept of "status politics."

members of the middle class and younger workers influenced by this class in terms of traditional values. In addition, there are people—entrepreneurs, executives, and higher-level civil servants—whose vested economic or personal interests in the *status quo* lead them to support the Liberal Democratic Party. Economic motivations among farmers, merchants, and small manufacturers, or even among manual workers, will also result in support for the Liberal Democratic Party. Such support is understandable, for, as the governing party, the Liberal Democrats can distribute various concrete rewards such as subsidies, construction of roads and bridges, tax cuts, and other legislative measures and executive actions. The attraction of these kinds of rewards seems to be increasing.[17] Yet there also exist vast psychological resources of traditional values which the Liberal Democrats can use, especially on occasions when such issues as education, labor, and police come to the forefront as political issues.

The Socialists depend on organized labor as the basis for organization and financing. Ideologically the Socialist Party claims that it is a class party representative of all laboring people. It is commonly regarded as the guardian of the interests of organized labor. Certainly it supports various welfare measures in order to establish itself as the guardian of all laboring and underprivileged people. However, its cause is weakened by the Liberal Democratic Party, which admits the necessity for such welfare measures, and whose welfare policies are incorporated into legislative statutes; thus the Liberal Democrats can boast of their achievements in this respect too. Even among organized laborers (or employees of big enterprises who are relatively favorably treated in comparison with those manual workers who are employed in medium- and small-size enterprises), support for the Socialists is not given

---

[17] Traditionally it was said that the three essential characteristics for successful candidates were the three *ban*: *jiban*, *kaban*, and *kanban*. *Jiban* meant solid territory, from which a candidate could expect firm support without much campaigning because of his status as a traditional notable there. *Kaban* meant a briefcase full of money for buying votes. *Kanban* meant a signboard, or the ability to impress one's name on the electorate. Today, instead of the three *ban*, people talk about the three *ki*: *rieki*, *soshiki*, and *ninki*. *Rieki* is benefits, *soshiki* is organization, and *ninki* is popularity. *Rieki* is definitely different from buying votes directly (*kaban*). It consists of distributing such benefits as government subsidies, construction of roads and bridges, and favorable legislation. These symbols are related to forms of support based on traditional ties and represent what Riesman refers to as "traditional types of apathy."

because of intense economic discontent or belief in the expected economic effects of a socialist regime.[18] Among the issues on which the Socialists and the Liberal Democrats have bitterly disagreed, noneconomic considerations have played an important role—e.g., the problem of revision of the 1947 Constitution and of various reform measures introduced after World War II, especially in the fields of education, police, and labor legislation. The Liberal Democrats have wanted to revise these in a direction more compatible with traditional values and, at the same time, in the direction of stronger, more centralized state power (particularly in the field of education). Some ultraconservative elements among the Liberal Democrats have been openly advocating more drastic revision of these measures than the leaders of the Liberal Democrats want to accept; this element among the Liberal Democrats has caused some support for the Socialists. The Socialist Party has vigorously opposed attempts to revise these reform measures, and many intellectuals have expressed strong opposition to such revision; we can say that the considerable support among white-collar workers for the Socialists is based on distrust of the Liberal Democrats concerning these matters.

Possible reasons for the importance of cultural politics or value politics are the following: (1) the existence of sharp cultural cleavages due to ethnic or religious heterogeneity in the society; (2) the rapid changes in society resulting in massive changes in values; (3) the relative economic prosperity (whereas economic discontent might motivate people to political participation); (4) the relative absence of status discontent due to rigid status demarcations.

Japan lacks the first condition, while in France and Italy, for example, the cleavage between clericalism and anticlericalism has plagued politics for a long time. The second condition is found in societies which are undergoing rapid modernization and indus-

---

[18]According to an opinion survey conducted among workers organized under Sōhyō (General Council of Trade Unions, a leftist national federation of labor unions) and Chūritsu-rōren (Federation of Independent Unions, which closely cooperates with Sōhyō), those who believed in the possibility of improvement in their living standards under a socialist regime numbered only 40 percent, while more than 60 percent voted for the Socialist Party. On the other hand, with regard to the revision of the 1947 Constitution, 90 percent were against the revision—that is, against the position of the Liberal Democratic Party. Quoted in Shinohara and Matsushita (1962).

trialization; in such cases, poverty, misery, and resentment toward rigid status demarcations inherited from previous periods usually play their roles in politics. However, in Japan, a broad basis for rational, antitraditional values and ideologies already developed long before World War II. For instance, the development of institutions for higher education was amazingly rapid long before World War II,[19] and the labor movement has a long history going back to the early twentieth century. Yet, officially, traditional or even mystical ancient values and ideologies had dominated (combined with ultranationalism and militarism), especially after 1930. After World War II, when restrictions on antitraditionalism were removed, antitraditional values, ideas, and ideologies gained momentum, and the spokesmen for such ideas took advantage of reform measures introduced by the Occupation authorities as the bulwark against the resistance and counterattack by the traditionalists. On the other hand, the traditionalists had reasons for wanting to revise post–World War II reform measures; they contended that most of these measures were imposed from outside and did not fit the "actual situation in Japan"; traditional values still strongly influenced rural sectors and older middle-class people in

[19] It has often been said that both the number of universities and the number of students enrolled in universities increased ten times as a result of post–World War II educational reforms. (At present there are 500 universities and colleges, including junior colleges, and 760,000 students.) As far as this statement concerns institutions legally recognized and formally designated as "university" or "college," it is correct. However, if we take into account various forms of higher-learning institutions which had existed before World War II and were reorganized as "universities" or as departments of a "university" after the war, the statement is misleading. For instance, in 1930, there were 230,000 students enrolled in 413 higher-learning institutions, as shown in the following table taken from the 1954 edition of the Ministry of Education's *Gakusei Hachijū Nenshi*:

	Number of institutions	Number of students
Universities	46	69,605
High schools[a]	32	20,551
Higher specialized training schools[b]	162	90,043
Various teachers' schools[c]	173	49,119
Total	413	229,318

[a]These were higher preparatory schools for later specialized studies in universities. Their character had much in common with liberal arts colleges in the United States.

[b]These were four-year schools, for which eleven years of previous education was required for entrance.

[c]During World War II the status of these teachers' schools was raised to the same level as that of higher specialized training schools, and after World War II, these were reorganized as teachers' colleges.

cities. Surely, they argued, it is a condition of stability to make legal institutions congruent with value patterns. Such strongly held views, based on a degree of support, contribute to the intensification of cultural politics in present-day Japan.

The status factor, as S. M. Lipset points out, has a bearing on the intensity of political conflict in society (*i.e.*, the more rigid the status demarcation line is, the more class-conscious people become). Japan is an interesting case to study in this regard. After the Meiji Restoration (1868), which abolished the feudal status, the new government created the legal status of nobility. It gave this status of nobility to ex-feudal lords, relatives and higher servants of the imperial family, and, later, to those military men, industrialists, and higher bureaucrats who had contributed to the regime, glorifying the nobility as the guardian group of the imperial family. Before World War II, in formal organizations, especially in government bureaucracy, a rigid distinction between higher and lower positions was established. The basic idea was that the higher the position, the closer it was to the emperor, and therefore the more it shared the glory of the emperor. In private enterprises, although such a mystique was lacking, the status demarcation between administrative personnel and workers was quite rigid, and hierarchical patterns defined every relationship within the formal organization. Even in the face of these strong and widespread status demarcations, nevertheless, the status system in prewar Japan had been fairly open. Whoever graduated from the imperial universities and passed the examination for higher governmental positions could expect to be promoted to high government office, almost regardless of birth status. Both in government bureaucracies and private enterprises, lower white-collar and manual workers could expect their sons to climb to higher status if they had higher education.[20] As for the nobility, it was a newly created status without tradition and reputation comparable to European nobilities; since this status was conferred on many generals, industrialists, and politicians, it was an achieved-honor system rather than an ascribed-status system.

---

[20]The Japanese word used in such a context is *gakureki*, which means one's "educational career." It refers to not merely the level of education, but also the particular school from which one graduated. It includes not only the quality of education at that school, but also the personal relationships among graduates from the same school.

After World War II, the nobility was legally abolished and economically badly stricken. Also, in formal organizations, strict demarcation of status considerably lessened. Although some privileged status positions and promotion routes still remain, the weakening of status lines is causing resentment among white-collar workers with lower "educational careers" and impelling them toward vigorous union activity. In coal mines and other industries, authoritarian labor management remains and stimulates militant union activity such as the "workshop struggle." However, in general, we should not attach much importance to status demarcations as stimuli for militant class politics. Certainly hierarchical interpersonal relationships remain strong everywhere, and we can see the pattern even within universities, labor unions, and the like, although they are weakened already and weakening more and more. The political consequence of hierarchical interpersonal relationships, which are part of traditional values, is the solidification of conservative support in the society. Thus, in Japan's case, status relationships do not greatly stimulate militant class-conscious action; on the contrary, they contribute to support of the Conservatives by large segments of the population.

As for the results of the emphasis on cultural politics, the following should be mentioned: generalization of issues and intensification of conflict. Clearly, in present-day Japanese politics, the issues are connected, interpreted, and perceived as part of a wider context of values, principles, and emotions. This occurs particularly concerning issues of education, police and other internal security, and labor legislation. Because of the generalized effect of cultural politics, conflicts are more intensified than they would be if factors of economic discontent and status were the only influences.[21] On the other hand, when cultural cleavage is superim-

---

[21] Some would prefer to explain this generalization of issues in terms of the prevalence of ideologies. For instance, in an article on Japanese politics, Passin (1962) put it as follows: "As in any country where politics is so ideological, compromise is difficult, and all issues tend to take on a total character. . . . No issue stands alone, to be dealt with piecemeal and *ad hoc*, but as part of a matrix of issues, interdependent and naturally reinforcing. . . . This quality of all-out, uncompromising struggle is the most disturbing feature of the political climate of Japan today."

I prefer the concept of cultural politics to ideological politics. Certainly cultural cleavage and ideological conflict reinforce each other, but it seems to me that cultural cleavage is the cause and ideological conflict is the effect. Moreover, although the leftists have a superabundance of ideologies strongly influenced by Marxist ideas, the Lib-

posed on intense economic discontent or status resentment, extreme political conflict, emotional and generalized, can result, and changes in total social structure can occur.

Prospects for the Future

The source of support for traditional values and also for the Liberal Democratic Party is the group of older citizens in the middle classes—small farmers and self-employed merchants and manufacturers—and also those who have low educational achievement levels. With changes in occupational structure, will the pattern of politics change? Again assuming all other things equal, two comments might be made: First, since the size of manual and white-collar groups will grow, and the size of the older middle class will decrease, the influence of white-collar and manual workers in the support of the Liberal Democrats should rise. This could bring about some change in a more "liberal" direction among the Liberal Democrats, because manual and white-collar workers who support them, however traditional or conservative in comparison with those who support the Socialists, are different from the old middle classes. They have interests in common with those manual and white-collar workers who support the Socialists. Second, it is probable that the Liberal Democrats, acknowledging this change in occupational structure, will have to begin to modernize party structure and activity. Already the necessity for such modernization has begun to be recognized by some leaders of the Liberal Democratic Party. However, there are factors which hinder the realization of such attempts. The supporters of the Liberal Democratic Party in local communities consist predominantly of old middle-class people; as changes threaten their position, they will become more conservative, even reactionary, being hostile to the organized workers (including the white-collar group). In view of the changing occupational structure, at least some of the leaders of the Liberal Democrats might become more "liberal," but

eral Democrats seem to be plagued by a lack of coherent ideology. Especially in the lower levels of the party, local subleaders and activists lack ideology, yet they "feel" deep distrust and even hatred toward what seems to be a destroyer of traditional values. They interpret Socialist opposition in terms of their traditional value frame, and they generalize the issues.

the grassroots activist subleader has little stimulus to become "liberal"; on the contrary, he has reason to be more conservative. Thus it is doubtful that the Liberal Democrats can extensively modernize their party structure and activity.[22] The Socialists seem content with the "natural" growth of support for their party, for the traditional and anti-intellectual aspect of the Liberal Democrats alienates white-collar workers, organized laborers, and more educated and younger people. However, to increase support beyond that "natural" tendency is particularly difficult for the Socialists, especially if the present economic prosperity continues. Since the psychological basis of support for the Socialists is largely inspired by distrust of the traditional and anti-intellectual position of the Liberal Democrats, the Socialists can gain more attention by radical rhetoric than by moderate views. Although the influence of orthodox Marxism on the ideology of the Socialists shows signs of weakening, the radical character of the ideology of the Socialists will not change in the near future.

Another important consideration affecting the pattern of future Japanese politics is the possibility of change in the political allegiance of the older members of the middle classes, especially the farmers. However far the process of industrialization in Japan proceeds, it is inconceivable that the size of the portion of the middle class would drop to the percentage demonstrated in Britain or the United States. The cases of Sweden and Norway provide a pattern in which conservative and traditional forces from the old middle class formed a particular interest group which exerted influence on government. Can we expect such a pattern in Japan's case? Can we expect farmers to become concerned about their particular economic interest because of the precarious position of agriculture in an industrial society—to establish a special-interest group, apart from the traditional and conservative political camp, and form some "neutral" camp? The pattern of politics would change totally and approach that of Scandinavia. Although there are some slight signs that Japanese farmers are becoming more benefit-conscious instead of tradition-bound, the probability or radical change in this direction is slight.

Needless to say, many factors are involved in any prediction of

---

[22] I have omitted discussion of the structures of Japanese political parties, since they have been discussed in detail by Scalapino and Masumi (1962).

future change in the pattern of politics in Japan.[23] I have attempted only to understand more fully some of these factors.

[23]For instance, one major factor that I have not discussed is the population structure. The drop in the birth rate and the extension of life expectancy is causing the ratio of older to younger people to change dramatically. How will the political allegiance of older people change? Will they cling to traditional values; become discontented because of alienation or poverty; or be contented with social welfare measures? Such changes will affect the relative strength of the Conservatives and the opposition parties, and also patterns of politics as a whole.

The most influential and unpredictable factor is an external one—the nature of the international situation. Generally speaking, a tense international situation can result in consensus formation or a lessening of internal conflict, or it can intensify existing internal political conflict. In Japan's case at present, the problems of foreign policy contribute to the intensification of political conflict—or, rather, they are used as a tool and expression of cultural politics.

Chapter 6
Intellectuals and the "Foreign Policy Public"

Within the general subject area of the role of intellectuals in foreign policy formation, I would like to focus on the relationship between foreign policy decision-makers and intellectuals, and try to pinpoint the variables which affect this relationship. We often find close links in developing societies between decision-makers and intellectuals. University presidents and professors are often appointed to top positions in government, and vice versa; even if there is no such occupational mobility, university professors are at least consulted by the government concerning policy formation in the fields of their specialities and can exercise far more influence than professors in other societies. As a matter of fact, in preparing a list of possible participants in a conference on "peace research in Asia," I was impressed with the fact that in many Asian countries scholars are deeply involved in high-level governmental affairs; many of the suggested names were those of people in governmental service.

The immaturity of professional bureaucratic structures and the scarcity of skilled personnel for top positions are important reasons for this mobility between top governmental positions and university positions, and for extensive influence by university professors on policy formation.

Does this mean that the intellectuals in those societies are performing a vital and decisive role in foreign policy formation? The answer depends upon the definitions employed and the expected role of intellectuals in a society. In defining intellectuals, the first thing mentioned usually is that the activities of intellectuals are connected with symbols—the creation, dissemination, and use of culture. Another characteristic which sometimes is regarded as essential to intellectuals is that they have a "detached concern" for their society and people (Coser, 1965). They try to be above blind involvement on the one hand and affected neutrality on the other. Therefore, a variety of opinions, hot debate, and dissent against dominant opinions are essential within the ranks of intellectuals.

Intellectuals and the Forum

The forums in which intellectuals can exchange views and disseminate their ideas have a variety of forms. Social clubs, professional associations, and the press all constitute forums for intellectuals. The press is especially important in terms of its influence and its capacity to support a number of intellectuals economically.

However, in societies where freedom of expression is not established, the press is the first target of government control. Because of censorship and threats of publication suspension, the press may tend to conform to governmental policy and become a mere organ of justifying and supporting it, or it may be tempted to stir up popular sentiments when they are congruent with the policies of the government or of some powerful faction of the government. It often happens that the press is more hawkish concerning foreign policy than the decision-maker because, first, the government usually esteems chauvinism above pacifism in the press, and, second, the reading public is fascinated by tough foreign policy stands. A good example of this occurred in Japan at the time of the Manchurian Incident in 1931. Foreign Minister Shidehara was suspicious of the action of the Japanese army and tried to limit it. However, all the major newspapers and magazines in Japan blamed China for causing the Incident and urged the necessity of taking determined action against China. And the Japanese military was determined to take over Manchuria by military action in spite of the restraint by foreign policy-makers. Thus, in this case, the press played on popular chauvinistic sentiments and supported the tough policy of the Japanese military, forcing the moderate foreign minister to resign his office four months after the occurrence of the Incident. Those Japanese intellectuals who were involved in the Japanese press at that time could boast that they exercised some influence on the adoption of a hawkish foreign policy toward China.

In defense of the position of the Japanese press in 1931, we could argue that at that time the press was not completely free from government control. However, the control was not so strict as in later years, particularly after 1936. The chauvinistic tone of the Japanese press in 1931 was the result not of governmental control but of voluntary expression—or at most self-regulated expression—of opinions by the journalists themselves.

Magazines seem better able than newspapers to survive government control and serve as a forum for dissenting opinions. They have smaller circulations and are oriented to narrower groups of readers. In Japan before World War II, the magazines could offer a wider variety of opinions and ideas than newspapers. When the Manchurian Incident occurred, such magazines as *Chūō kōron* and *Kaizō* were not chauvinistic at all. Although the rhetoric used was cautiously modified in order to pass through the government censorship, and sometimes words or sentences were deleted, *Kaizō* in particular was still able to publish a variety of articles critical of the Japanese military and government. There was a sequel, however. The publication of *Kaizō* was suspended and its editorial staff was arrested in 1943.

Para-Intellectuctuals and Popular Sentiments

In examining pre–World War II Japan, where the press stirred up popular chauvinistic sentiments, Maruyama Masao (1963) introduced the distinction between elite intellectuals and para-intellectuals (or secondary intellectuals). Elite intellectuals were those educated in higher educational institutions and imbued with Western thought. Some were liberal and others were under the strong influence of Marxism. They were the main audience for such highbrow journals as the aforementioned *Chūō kōron* and *Kaizō*, and also publications from the Iwanami Publishing Company. In contrast with them, para-intellectuals were those who had advanced to a middle level of education; their orientation was nativist and nationalist, and they were in positions of influence in local communities. They constituted the audience for the mass press (in this connection, it would be appropriate to note that in Japan there has been no distinction between quality newspapers and mass ones) and for popular writings such as those published by the Kōdansha Publishing Company. Someone has argued that in pre–World War II Japan there existed two kinds of culture—one was highbrow Iwanami culture and another was popular Kōdansha culture.

Does this distinction between elite intellectuals and para-intellectuals apply to other societies as well? It depends on various factors. Speaking of para-intellectuals, first, supposes a fairly high level of literacy and education among the general populace. Second, it presupposes the existence of nativistic and nationalistic intellectual traditions. And, third, there must be some isolation of elite intellectuals (whose higher education included introduction to Western ideas and thought—and technology—in a liberal atmosphere) from those whose middle-level education consisted more of instruction in traditional and nativistic ideas and a disciplinary code of behavior.

In Japan's case, this kind of dual structure of intellectuals has disappeared rapidly since World War II, due to the enormous expansion of higher education and the reforms at middle levels of the educational system. In contemporary Japan there is no clear discrepancy between intellectuals and nonintellectuals, but a hazy continuity between the two. In other words, there is no longer a sharp distinction between the Iwanami and Kōdansha cultures.

In other societies, especially those of developing countries, the normal pattern seems to be a dichotomy between intellectuals and nonintellectuals. As mentioned above, in these cases the elite intellectuals are fused with the decision-makers.

However, the pre–World War II Japanese pattern of stratification of intellectuals into elite Western-oriented intellectuals and para-intellectuals with nativist and nationalistic orientations might be found in some developing societies where nativist intellectual traditions are strong (for example, Muslim societies). If that is so, the actions and opinions of those para-intellectuals will require more attention in any attempt to understand the relationship between the intellectuals and policy formation.

Intellectuals and Public Opinion

In advanced, democratic societies where there is freedom of expression, a developed mass media, and high levels of education, public opinion exists in the sense that there are people who have interests and opinions concerning certain public issues. In order to analyze the role of intellectuals in foreign policy formation, we have to inquire into, first, the position and role of intellectuals within public opinion on foreign policy, and second, the relationship between foreign policy-makers and public opinion.

Generally speaking, in an age of public opinion and in societies with developed mass media and high educational levels, virtually every person and every group can be vocal on any issue. The definition and the scope of the intellectual class becomes inevitably vague. Therefore, we can give only a vague answer to the question of who makes public opinion. As Rosenau (1961, pp. 59–73) has pointed out, there are a variety of opinion-makers, governmental, institutional, associational, and individual. Intellectuals, as individuals, are just one type. In addition, intellectuals can represent or even be hired by opinion-makers from institutional and associational groups.

However, not every person or group is concerned with every issue. Depending on the area or country toward which the foreign policy is directed, as well as the degree of politicization of the issue, the scope of the "public" involved seems to be different. Therefore, it would be useful to try to determine the "foreign policy public" in relation to certain issues (and their domestic politicization), areas, or countries, and to pinpoint the weight and role of intellectuals in each individual case. A point worth considering in this connection seems to be the relationship between the military and business circles (or those intellectuals who are representing either of them) and those free and detached intellectuals in the foreign policy public concerned about some particular issue, area, or country. In the case of Japan since World War II, business circles have been an especially powerful segment of the foreign policy public. In other countries, especially the U.S., the weight of the military in the foreign policy public is very high.

In democracies with freedom of expression and developed mass media, the vocalness of opinions does not necessarily correspond to the effectiveness of those opinions in influencing policies. The establishment of particular foreign policies depends more on the dynamics of parliamentary politics and bureaucratic dynamics, as Allison (1969) has argued.

Discussing the role of intellectuals in foreign policy formation, or any policy formation, the questions of who are the intellectuals and what is their role in society remain. If we emphasize "detached concern" as the essential characteristic of intellectuals, their role is not to serve policy formation but rather to always remain somewhat "alienated from power." From this viewpoint, "policy intellectuals" would themselves be a contradiction in terms. Intellectuals would be expected to exchange opinions and views—including those of dissenting voices—in their own forums and to appeal to the public. In other words, through their influence on public opinion, intellectuals would watch over the moves of decision-makers and check their errors.

In contrast with this, if we define the intellectual as a creator, disseminator, and applier of culture (cf. Lipset, 1960, p. 333) then, in relation to the topic discussed here, we should pay more attention to the role of social science experts in policy formation. A more specific point to be considered would be the relationship between high-ranking bureaucrats and social scientists. Important points to be considered would be whether the top positions in a bureaucracy are open to social scientists, and, if not, whether professional bureaucrats are ready to accept advice and proposals from social scientists.

Part III

Japan in Asia and the World

Chapter 7
Nation-Building at the Edge of an Old Empire

Compared to the rest of the world, China, Korea, and Japan all developed distinctive politicocultural systems remarkably early.

In the case of China, such distinctiveness can be traced back to the Chou (1122–255 B.C.) and the Ch'in (255–206 B.C.) dynasties. Chinese characters, Confucianism and other Chinese philosophies that influenced not only the Chinese people but also the Koreans and the Japanese until the nineteenth or even the twentieth century; the idea of the "Middle Kingdom," which contained the assumption of the cultural unity and supremacy of China over "external barbarians"—all these were the products of the period of the Chou dynasty. In terms of political integration, the first emperor of the Ch'in dynasty, Shih Huang Ti, took such important steps as the creation of a centralized administrative organization; the unification of weights and measures; and the construction of roads leading to the capital, canals connecting north and south, and the famous Great Wall that constituted part of the boundary of its empire. As for administrative organization, it was nearly a thousand years later, under the T'ang dynasty (A.D. 618–907), that the next decisive development occurred: the founding emperor of the T'ang, T'ai Tsung, set up the famous civil-service examination system, the rudimentary form of which can be traced as far back as the Han (206 B.C.–A.D. 220), making it the sole channel to all official positions; he also effected an elaborate reorganization of the central and local administrative establishments. (As will be noted later, the T'ang's political institutions served as a model in both Korea and Japan.) The basic cultural unit and home of the Chinese (Han) people was the Middle Kingdom, which has continuously expanded through their migrations and conquests. Since the Middle Kingdom has been basically a cultural definition rather than an ethnic or geographical one, its physical boundary has remained vague. However, because of this cultural definition, political conquests by non-Han rulers—the most durable ones were those by the Mongols in the period of the Yüan dynasty (A.D. 1206–1368) and by the Manchu in that of the Ch'ing dynasty (1644–1911)— have not affected Chinese cultural (and, consequently, political) continuity and unity, into which such minority rulers have been absorbed.

In the case of Korea, the date of political unification can be traced back to A.D. 670 when the Silla kingdom came to encompass the whole region of Korea. This political unification was maintained and developed through the succeeding Koryŏ (918– 1392) and Yi (1392–1910) dynasties, in spite of occasional invasions from the north (by the Chinese of the Sui and T'ang dynasties in the seventh century, the Khitan in the late tenth and early eleventh, the Mongols of the Yüan Empire in the thirteenth and fourteenth centuries) and from the south (the Japanese under Hideyoshi in the late sixteenth century). Thus, in 957 under the Koryŏ dynasty, a civil-service examination system was instituted, and later under the Yi dynasty it was elaborated and perfected. The Yi dynasty seems to have achieved a high degree of centralized bureaucratic rule. In terms of cultural unity, Korea, like Japan, has enjoyed almost complete ethnic and linguistic homogeneity from the beginning of its history. The spoken language has been one with no dialects except that of Choju Do, an island to the south of the Korean peninsula. A system of writing the Korean language using Chinese ideography was used from the fourth to the fifteenth centuries, until the Korean alphabet, *hangul*, was devised. Thereafter, although many Chinese characters continued to be used, writing based on *hangul* spread gradually.

In Japan's case, historians agree that initial political unification was achieved around the fifth century and reinforced in the seventh century when Prince Shōtoku launched the Taika reform (A. D. 645), and the Taihō code was promulgated (A. D. 700) (Inoue, 1960). The ensuing periods—the Nara (710–793) and Heian (794–1192) periods, named after their respective capitals (Heian is the ancient name for Kyoto)—are sometimes referred to as those of the *ritsu-ryō* system or the *ritsu-ryō* state, meaning a uniform and centralized state under the emperor (*tennō*) by law (*ritsu*) and code (*ryō*). Before that time, the *tennō* was the head of the most powerful clan, and his power and authority were restricted by the existence and autonomy of other clans. The Taika reform and Taihō code aimed at and achieved, to a certain degree, the restriction of the power of other clans by abolishing all the great private holdings of land and by setting up a uniform and centralized administrative apparatus. The T'ang system in China was considered exemplary in these reforms. Ethnically speaking, in spite of the existence of various clans, Japan already seems to have enjoyed a high degree of ethnic homogeneity over most of its territory, the sole exception being the northern part of Honshū where clashes with an alien tribe called the Ezo were recorded in the eighth and ninth centuries (whether the Ezo were the forebears of the present Ainu living in Hokkaido has not yet been determined). At that time, Hokkaido was an unknown land to the Japanese. As in Korea, one language was spoken from the beginning of the known period. In developing its written language, Japan took over the Chinese ideography, rapidly making the necessary modifications, and in the early Heian period Japanese syllable letters were developed. During the Heian period much literature was written using these Japanese letters—literature that is still read, the most famous example being the *Genji monogatari* (*The Tale of Genji*), written in the early eleventh century.

In Japan, political unification and centralization did not go as far as in China and Korea. Under the Taika reform, local administrative units such as provinces (*kuni*) and counties (*gun*) were established, the heads of which were appointed by the central government. However, it was quite symbolic of the lesser degree of political unification in Japan that, as Burks mentions,

> the Japanese term for the province, *kuni*, uses the same ideograph as the Chinese character *kuo*, which to the Chinese means realm, kingdom, or country. The scattered topography of Japan and the tradition of clan independence made it easy for the Japanese to think of their newly reformed Empire as a composite of many small realms (Linebarger, Chu, and Burks, 1967, p. 287).

No civil-service examination system after the Chinese model was attempted. Finally, the Heian period ended in a struggle between two warrior clans and the establishment by the victorious clan of a kind of military government in Kamakura (1193). From 1193 to the end of the Edo (Tokugawa) period, a dual government was maintained: while the emperor, the court, and the nobles were in Kyoto going through the ceremonial motions of ruling, the actual ruler was the generalissimo (*shōgun*). The first holder of this title, appointed by the emperor, was the leader of the most powerful warrior group, but the title became hereditary, remaining in the same family until a rival group managed to usurp control. The Tokugawa shogunate, maintaining its capital in Edo (Tokyo), lasted for 265 years with fifteen successive inheritors of the *shōgun* position. Even the shogunate, however, did not achieve complete centralization. Under the Tokugawa shogunate, which was the most stable and centralized compared to those preceding it, there were 260–70 feudal lords (*daimyō*) with their own territory over which they exercised a fairly autonomous rule in spite of certain regulations imposed by the shogunate.

The impact of the West in the nineteenth century and the necessity for modernization made it impossible for the traditional system to survive in any of the countries of East Asia. The Ch'ing dynasty in China, the Yi dynasty in Korea, and the Tokugawa shogunate in Japan all collapsed. After the collapse, however, these three followed quite different routes to modernization. The most tragic case was Korea, which had taken various measures to cope with the external pressures and to bring about modernization. In 1882 it adopted what is still the national flag of the Republic of Korea, the *Taegukki*, and various attempts at reform were made: the Taewongun reform of 1867, the Kaewadang reform of 1884, the Tonghak rebellion of 1894, and the Independence Club movement of 1896–98. Nevertheless, Korea became a pawn in the international struggles of the Western states and China and Japan. It was finally annexed by Japan in 1910, ceasing to exist as an independent political unit for the next thirty-five years. In China, the final and belated fall of the Ch'ing dynasty in 1911 was followed by political chaos; provincial warlords (*tuchuns*) played prominent roles, especially in the north, for over a decade, until the Kuomintang brought about political unification in 1927 under the "sun-in-the-blue-sky" flag. In contrast to China and Korea, the downfall of the Tokugawa shogunate in Japan was followed by the expeditious formation of the Meiji state and rapid progress in modernization.

Looking at the different routes followed by these three East Asian countries into the modern world, one is impressed by the fact that a long, historical existence as a cultural and political unity *per se* was not a sufficient condition for building and developing a nation or state capable of surviving and developing in the modern world. From these examples, one is led to raise the following questions: what were the factors that made it possible to build a viable nation in Meiji Japan, and what were the factors that hindered the same development in China and Korea? Concerning the first question, a number of analyses and arguments have been presented by both Japanese and non-Japanese scholars.[1] Several studies have tried to compare the case of Japan with that of other countries—Britain and France (Kuwabara, 1964; Kawano, 1961; Ueyama, 1968), Germany (Bendix, 1964), and Turkey (Ward and Rustow, 1964). However, there has been no study comparing the three countries in East Asia in terms of political modernization or modern nation-building. There are some studies referring to China and Japan,[2] but no comparative studies including Korea, so far as the author knows, although there are an increasing number of studies on Korean political development.[3]

To the second question, the answer can be sought in two approaches. One is to look into internal factors in China and Korea which hindered or at least delayed the development of a viable nation in the modern period. The studies by Levy (1955) and Henderson (1968) can be regarded as such efforts. Another is to see external factors as the main cause of failure. Thus, Japan's rapid formation of the Meiji state and subsequent development di-

[1] The study of the Meiji Restoration and the nation-building following it has attracted many Japanese historians and social scientists. A vast amount of material on this topic has been published in Japanese (see Rekishigaku Kenkyūkai, 1958, 1969). An example of study on this topic by non-Japanese scholars is Ward (1968).

[2] The classic example by a Japanese scholar is Hani (1948), which was originally published as journal articles in 1932 and is a comparative study of Japan, China, and India focusing on politicoeconomic modernization. More recent examples in English are Holt and Turner (1966) and Levy (1955). Holt and Turner examine four cases—those of England, France, China, and Japan, focusing on the takeoff stage of economic growth.

[3] Three publications are especially relevant to the topic of nation-building and political modernization: Lee (1963), Lee (1968), and Henderson (1968).

rectly affected China and Korea. On the one hand, some regarded Japan as a model of development for China and Korea, but on the other hand, Japan's annexation of Korea, possession of Taiwan, and invasion of Manchuria undeniably showed that Japan was the direct enemy of the independence and political unity of China and Korea. Studies of East Asian political history between 1868 and 1945 are full of descriptions and analyses of Japan's impact on China and Korea—that is, the negative impact of the development of one political unit in the region on the political development of other units, or, to put it in another way, the consequences of unbalanced political development within the region.

Viewed in this way, one can doubt whether Japan between 1868 and 1945 is an example of political development in the positive sense. As a matter of fact, not only Barrington Moore (1966) but others also—especially Japanese scholars—regard the political development of Japan from 1868 to 1945 and especially from 1930 to 1945 as the development of Asian fascism or ultranationalism or capitalistic imperialism or something else negative.[4] Others attempt, as S. N. Eisenstadt (1966) did, to introduce such concepts as breakdown or decay of modernization in order to explain Japan's external actions and internal structure, especially from 1930 to 1945.

Necessary Conditions for State-Building

So far I have focused on the given historical, cultural, and political situation in each of the three countries. The important question to be asked is: What were the conditions necessary for building a viable nation or state that could coexist with the other na-

[4] See Moore (1966). Moore's perspective on the problem differs from that found in most discussions of political modernization or nation-building. As the title of the book (*Social Origins of Dictatorship and Democracy*) indicates, the question Moore raises is: What are the factors that lead to different routes and to different political forms in the modern world? He points to three routes. The first is a combination of capitalism and parliamentary democracy achieved after a series of revolutions; the second is a combination of capitalism and a succession of reactionary political structures culminating in fascism; and the third is communism. Moore puts Japan in the second category, analyzing it under the title "Asian Fascism."

A large number of articles and books in Japanese take this sort of tone. In 1955, a book that severely criticized Japanese development in the Shōwa era (1926–) was published and attained a wide circulation (Tōyama, Imai, and Fujiwara, 1955).

tions in the modern world? In these terms, the historical existence of cultural and political unity is not sufficient; in fact, it can be counterproductive.

Take the example of China. The idea of the Middle Kingdom, which had been the symbol of the cultural and political unity of China, functioned in the nineteenth century to encourage an unrealistic and suicidal response to the Western powers. Chinese political leaders, mesmerized by the concept of the Middle Kingdom, found little to learn from the West, rejecting technological progress; they even treated the diplomatic delegation from the victorious British as a tributary mission, making realistic diplomacy impossible. In China's case, as has often been pointed out, in spite of long political centralization and cultural unity, the family and kinship had provided the focus of loyalty for the vast population living in villages; loyalty to the family and kinship transcended all other social obligations. Perhaps we should say "because of long cultural unity and centralization" instead of "in spite of . . . ." Confucian philosophy, which constituted part of the cultural unity of traditional China, endorsed such a family-centered standard of morality. Political centralization seems to have been facilitated by a social and moral vacuum beyond the family and kinship level; the rulers did not attempt to mobilize mass support, being content with the chance of ruling with relatively small forces as a result of the vacuum.[5]

In order to analyze the causes of Korea's failure to build a viable nation or state in the nineteenth century, we must not ignore the external factors—especially the threats from Japan and the final annexation by Japan in 1910. However, if we engage in a

[5] Cf. Levy (1955). As Yang (1959, pp. 173–74) writes: "All modern Chinese reformers have tried to shift the center of loyalty from the family to the state. K'ang Yu-wei in his *Ta T'ung Shu* (The Great Commonwealth) pointed out the incompatibility between family loyalty and national interest. Sun Yat-sen in his *San-min Chu-i* (Three People's Principles) exhorted his countrymen to broaden familism to nationalism by widening the center of loyalty from the family to the nation. The defeats China had suffered from foreign powers made the adoption of nationalism and patriotism a matter of urgent necessity. The Japanese invasion and the ensuing eight years of devastating war (1937–45) extended the influence of nationalism from the intelligentsia to other classes of the population. The state as a morally higher center of loyalty had been an established factor in the modern trend of social, economic, and political events prior to the rise of the Communist regime, but in no previous period has the interest of the state . . . been more sharply defined and loyalty to it been more drastically demanded than under the Communist rule."

kind of speculative experiment and assume for the moment that the external threats were small or nonexistent, we can ask whether Korea could have built and developed a viable nation-state anyway, taking advantage of its ethnic, linguistic, and political unity.

One is tempted to give an affirmative answer to this question, considering such characteristics of the Korean society and people as the spread of education, their diligence, and so on, in addition to their ethnic, linguistic, and political unity. However, Gregory Henderson (1968, pp. 4–5) develops a rather paradoxical logic: "because of" ethnic, linguistic, and political unity, a political dynamic he calls "the politics of vortex" was generated and resulted in factionalism, indecision, and lack of political leadership. Let us follow Henderson's logic a little further:

> I argue here that the unity and homogeneity of Korea acted to produce a *mass* society, much, perhaps, as they acted for the population of the core area of her neighbor, China. By mass society, I mean a society lacking in the formation of strong institutions or voluntary associations between village and throne; a society that knows little of castle town, feudal lord and court, semi-independent merchant societies, city-states, guilds, or classes cohesive enough to be centers of independent stance and action in the polity.
>
> . . . Compactness of the territory, absence of ethnic, religious, political, linguistic, or other basic sources of cleavage within Korea, and a universalistic value system have created a society in which groupings are artificial.
>
> . . . Grouping is hence an opportunistic matter concerned only with access to power for its members, and, because other differences are not present, each group tends to be distinguished from the others only by the personalities of its members and by their relationship to power at the time. Hence groupings are factional; for the issues and interests that forge true parties from factions are absent from the homogeneous, power-bent society. . . . The result is a pattern of extreme centripetal dynamics. . . . The physics of Korean political dynamics appears to resemble a strong vortex tending to sweep all active elements of the society upward toward central power. . . . Intermediary groupings find it difficult to achieve aggregation. Vertiginous updraft tends to suck

all components from each other before they cohere on lower levels and tends to propel them in atomized form toward the power apex.

As Henderson himself admits, this is a very bold, ambitious, and provocative theory to use in comparing China, Korea, and Japan. Also it has tremendous significance for the theory of nation-building and political development. As Henderson hints, we have to raise the question: "Is it possible that the unity, centrality, and homogeneity now sought by emerging nations may set in motion, as they did for Korea, a vortex similarly destructive to political amalgamation and pluralism?" Or as Samuel P. Huntington put it in the foreword to Henderson's book, we might be able to propose a more general proposition saying that "what is good for national integration is not necessarily good for national development." Let us examine Henderson's "Korea—mass society—politics of vortex" theory, taking into consideration China and Japan for comparison. As for China, in the above quotation Henderson seems to regard it too as a "mass society" in his sense, and we might infer, therefore, that to use Henderson's expression, China would be regarded as having been caught in the politics of vortex, resulting in factionalism, indecision, incompetent political leadership, and inability to build a viable nation. Certainly that was proved by the history of the late Ch'ing dynasty in the nineteenth and early twentieth centuries. However, I hesitate very much to use the mass society concept in this context, for it is also used in contemporary sociology, where it denotes the existence of atomized individuals, subject to easy manipulation by the state or ruling minority. In other words, the basic assumption is complete penetration by the state or the ruling elite into the mass of atomized individuals, and a high degree of modern manipulation through state-sponsored organizations and media made possible by modern techniques of communication. To apply the same concept to a traditional, centralized society inevitably causes confusion. Take the example of the Chinese and Korean societies of the nineteenth century, where apparently the unit was not the individual, but the family or kin group. Penetration by the central government or by a ruling elite was not complete in the modern sense, because the techniques of manipulation were not available. To apply the concept of mass society to this sort of situation seems impossible. In terms of social relationships, people in those societies were not scattered, isolated individuals, but were tightly drawn into small social units of family, kin group, and village. Thus there was a peculiar combination of traditional segmentation and centralization. In this sense, we might use the concept of traditional mass society.

Viewed in terms of this theory of a traditional mass society, and contrasting Japan with Korea, what were the characteristics of Japanese society in the premodern period, and what were their consequences? In scattered and occasional references to Japan, Henderson in his book points to the existence of more regional differentiation and specialization than in Korea, to the existence of a more pronounced hierarchy, and to the greater prevalence of upward loyalty. Certainly these were characteristics of Japan's Tokugawa society, because it was a feudal society in which the feudal lords had their own territories, demanded that their vassals pay homage to them, and attempted to get more revenue by encouraging or manipulating commerce and industry within their territories. On the other hand, because it was a centralized feudalism, the political unity of Japan as a whole was maintained, and trade and commerce developed on a nationwide scale. In addition, the emperor served as the magnet for feelings of unity, and served as a renewed source of the legitimacy of political power when the Tokugawa shogunate fell.

In Japan's case, both of those elements (feudal regionalism and centralization) happened to be so arranged that they facilitated nation-building after the Meiji Restoration of 1868. However, it was not so much the mere existence of these elements as the conscious manipulation of them that was important for the Meiji nation-building. We must therefore pay more attention to that manipulation, which on the one hand contributed to rapid nation-building in Korea and China.

As is often pointed out, the manipulative measures taken in Meiji Japan were peculiar; they succeeded in transforming the traditional attachment to family, kin group, and village to loyalty to the nation by means of the doctrine and myth of a "family state" led by the emperor. Utilizing loyalty to feudal lords and the spiritual authority of the imperial family, these measures caused traditional and somewhat primitive attachments to primary groups and the immediate environment to be linked to loyalty to the emperor and the state. This proved to be a highly successful short cut to the building of a viable nation ("a prosperous nation and a strong military" as the Meiji leaders said), but at the same time it revealed its own contradictions and strains. Internally, since the political power of the Meiji state was legitimized by the spiritual authority of the emperor and implemented by the bureaucratic apparatus, power tended to invade the private and spiritual world of the citizens and to forestall any participation or control by the people. As a matter of fact, in the "family state" ideas and practices associated with civil liberties and popular participation were not fully recognized, and finally in the "Imperial state" of Japan in the 1940s they were declared to be without value.[6] Only after the defeat in World War II, and in the presence of the Allied Occupation Forces, could Japan rebuild its state in a form fully compatible with civil liberties and popular participation.

Japan's external behavior between 1868 and 1945 can be explained in various ways and certainly reflects multiple causes. However, given the present purpose of identifying the consequences of the Meiji way of nation-building, we have to pay special attention to the nature of Meiji nationalism and its grotesque outgrowth, the ultranationalism of the Imperial state during World War II; for nationalism as an ideology, an integrative political symbol, and a popular sentiment was and is one of the important factors in nation-building. As Maruyama (1963) points out, the first thing to be noticed is the lack of a sense of membership in an international community in the East Asia of the nineteenth century.[7] In spite of long historical contacts among China,

---

[6] In its 1941 *The Ways of the Subject*, the Ministry of Education, said: "What we normally refer to as 'private life' is, in the final analysis, the way of the subject. As such, it has a public significance, in that each so-called private action is carried out by the subject as part of his humble efforts to assist the Throne. . . . Thus we must never forget that even in our personal lives we are joined to the Emperor and must be moved by the desire to serve our country" (quoted in Maruyama, 1963, p. 7).

[7] Before the modern nation-state was born, Europe had already established one form of universalism. The foundations had been laid by the Roman Empire, which bequeathed its ideas to the doctrine of a European corporate body—the Corpus Christum—symbolized by the Roman Catholic (Universal) Church and the Holy Roman Empire. The development of modern nation-states beginning in the Renaissance and Reformation periods was no more than a pluralistic disruption that had originally been one. National consciousness in Europe therefore bore from its inception the

Korea, and Japan (and partly because of the seclusion policy of
Yi Korea and Tokugawa Japan, both of which closed their doors
to foreigners for over two hundred years) there was no sense of
international community even among these three. Moreover, the
traditional Chinese concept of the Middle Kingdom, applied to
international relations, was based on the idea of superior and inferior relationships between nations, especially in cultural terms.
Faced with threats from the Western powers, all three East Asian
countries—China, Korea, and Japan—reacted in a similar way
to the initial impact. The rulers in all three, believing in the superiority of their own nation, showed a strong sense of repugnance for
the West. "Repel the barbarians" was commonly used as a slogan
in all three. Once defeated by the overwhelming military strength
of the Western powers, the rulers of the three countries soon recognized the need to learn and absorb from the West. In this
respect, too, all three reacted in similar ways. Distinguishing between the material and the spiritual, the technical and the cultural, and believing in the cultural superiority of their own nations,
the rulers tried to take from the West only the material, the technological, and the military. The point is that this sort of situation
led the ruling group in Japan, and also, to a considerable degree,
the people, to see the world as an arena, a power struggle, where
there were conquerors and conquered, superiors and inferiors.
According to this view, and due to the lack of a sense of community among the three East Asian countries, the Japanese, after
their success in nation-building and industrialization following the
Meiji Restoration, began to think that Korea and China were
inferior and were there to be conquered. Supported by this sort of
logic and popular sentiment, the Meiji state annexed Korea. It
also intervened in China in the second decade of the twentieth
century after the downfall of the Ch'ing dynasty, among other
things making demands on China in 1915 in the form of twenty-
one points. After 1930, this sort of Japanese view of international
relations was combined with the idea of the family state and the

imprint of a consciousness of international society. It was a self-evident premise that
disputes among sovereign states were conflicts among independent members of this
international society. . . . How does this compare with the so-called Asian world?
It is . . . clear that the nations of the East have never constituted a corporate body of
international society in the European sense, although various forms of diplomatic
intercourse have existed among them (Maruyama, 1963, pp. 138–39).

Imperial Way and developed into that notorious idea of a Greater East Asia Co-Prosperity Sphere. According to this idea, Japan was supposed to be the leader or the father of Asian nations. Inside this sphere, a hierarchical relationship among the states was assumed; and outside this sphere, the rule of the conqueror and the conquered, the strong and the weak, was supposed to work.

Implications of the East Asian Cases

What are the implications for the theory of nation-building? The East Asian cases suggest the following points. First, what the three countries experienced in common was the impact of the Western powers in the latter part of the nineteenth century. I have not discussed the nature of the Western powers at that time, but it is quite apparent that they did not behave in a way favorable either to the maintenance of the traditional political unity of these countries or to their rebuilding in modern form. In dealing with the problems of nation-building, we have to take into consideration this sort of world situation.

Second, the East Asian cases give us an example of unbalanced development among neighboring units within a region. This unbalanced development had an unfortunate consequence in that the most successful unit terminated the independent existence of one neighbor and impeded development in another through intervention. Attention must be given to this sort of political dynamics within a region and between neighboring units, and its causes and consequences assessed.

Third, Japan's seemingly successful attempt at nation-building after the Meiji Restoration—if we take into consideration the internal and external consequences of that mode of nation-building —suggests that there is a grave danger in making too great a use of the traditional social structure and ancient myths (such as Japan's emperor myth) in modern nation-building, and that nationalism or national consciousness should be combined with some elements of internationalism or belief in the existence of an international community. Given the world situation of the late nineteenth century, Japan was perhaps justified in adopting the goal of a prosperous nation and a strong military. But, if so, it only meant that a later rebuilding and reorientation was imperative if Japan was to accept equality as a basis of its relations with its East Asian neighbors and if it was to permit civil liberties and popular participation in government at home. Actually, in Japan's case, some move toward such rebuilding appeared during the 1920s. Externally, Foreign Minister Shidehara Kijūrō, who served successively in five cabinets from 1924 to 1931, supported a policy of nonintervention toward China. Internally, universal manhood suffrage was introduced in 1925 and the Party Cabinet based on the majority in the Diet emerged in 1924. However, as is well known, these moves touched off countermoves from the political forces and values built into the Meiji state. The result was the emergence of the Imperial state, which was a grotesquely developed form of the Meiji state. The rebuilding and reorientation finally took place only after complete defeat in World War II.

Fourth, the (traditional) mass society theory presented by Henderson breaks down into the following elements:

1. As is often pointed out, the political rule of the traditional Chinese (and Korean) dynasties was a combination of centralization at the top and decentralized agrarian village communities at the bottom. This rule differed from the rule of feudalism in both Western Europe and Japan, where there was considerable decentralization; it also differed from the political rule of the centralized ancient empires, such as the Roman Empire or the Egyptian Empire, which were characterized by the direct use of slave labor on large estates of the *latifundium* type. This fact has been repeatedly pointed out by Karl Marx and others. In this respect, Henderson's theory is another attempt to focus on, and assess the consequences of, the vacuum or gap between political centralization and self-sufficient village life.

2. However, if we focus on village life and trace its effects on political culture even in today's Japan, we find several features similar to those that Henderson attributed to the historical existence of (traditional) mass society. My point is that these features, such as lack of association, prevalence of factionalism, and so on, can be found in Japan, too (cf. Ishida, 1968), which has not been the (traditional) mass society in Henderson's sense. Therefore, the historical origin of these features should be sought in the behavior patterns nourished in villages with their small-scale farming

methods, close social relationships, and communal character. Stated more generally, the question is how democracy, which emphasizes individual rights, can develop in Asian societies having a communal political culture based on small-scale farming and agrarian village life.

3. As for ethnic linguistic and cultural homogeneity, certainly in Japan's case too this was one of the factors that contributed to the rapid building of a centralized state after the Meiji Restoration. As a matter of fact, after World War II, when the rebuilding of the nation was attempted with emphasis on local autonomy, a strong tendency toward uniform and centralized administration persisted and later revived. From the viewpoint of encouraging local autonomy and grassroots democracy, this sort of homogeneity can have some disadvantages. We can also argue that the existence of a certain degree of heterogeneity can contribute toward checking excessive centralization if properly handled (cf. Lijphart, 1969).

Fifth, looking at contemporary East Asia as a whole, we become aware of particular problems. One is the existence of historical societies divided into more than one state. Korea is a typical example, and China shares the same problem. However, in the case of China there exist some ethnic minorities, and geographical and social boundaries are still somewhat vague, especially on its western frontier. In addition, the large number of Chinese living in various countries in Southeast Asia poses very important problems with regard to nation-building and political development. The different facets of the problem of overseas Chinese deserve special attention and research in both a theoretical and a practical sense.[8] Apart from China's special features, the existence of divided states reminds us again to take the world situation into consideration in dealing with the problem of nation-building.

The second problem in East Asia is the weakness of the sense of an international community, shared by the political units of the region, which might keep them compatible and contribute to their

---

[8] Eberhard (1968) and Collings (1968) both argue, taking the example of historical Chinese society, that the concept of social system or political system is difficult to apply to societies with vague boundaries. Collings proceeds to advance a "historical sociology" approach that analyzes society or politics in terms of interest groups and layers, without assuming the interrelationship of all the elements of society or any boundaries.

common development. Various factors have produced this situation. Historically, it traces back to the premodern era, and has been accentuated by Japan's external behavior since the Meiji era, especially towards Korea. In addition, tensions arising from the creation of divided states in the area after World War II are another factor. However, in this respect, other regions in the world are plagued with a similar problem. Its solution requires both prudent action by each nation concerned and research by social scientists.

Problems for Further Research

Generally speaking, whenever we try to undertake a comparative study of this sort, we are bothered by the limited amount of knowledge and data available. In particular, there is, as Rokkan (1969) points out, a tendency toward "large nation bias," so that very little information about small units is available in the international scholarly world. In the case of East Asia, a fairly large amount of information is available about China and Japan, but not enough for sophisticated comparative studies. Quite inadequate knowledge about Mongolia and Korea is available to scholars who are not specialists in these areas but who want to make comparative studies encompassing these countries. To improve and advance the field of comparative studies, we need to accumulate and codify the social histories particularly of the smaller units in the world.

Another question concerns the advantages and disadvantages of proceeding by regions in accumulating our comparative knowledge. The advantages are the following: (1) this method provides the opportunity to take into consideration the small units that otherwise are often ignored; (2) it compels researchers to give their attention to the various interactions among the units in the region and the resulting consequences; and (3) the units in the same region often have some similarities in terms of their internal social and cultural structures. Therefore, intraregional comparison can provide useful clues for interregional or worldwide comparison.

However, the definition of a region cannot avoid some vagueness and arbitrariness. Take the example of East Asia. Naturally East

Asia has not been and is not an isolated region. Historically, through succeeding Chinese empires, it has had contact and interaction with other regions, and more recently Japan's action in World War II has had important effects on the nation-building of various units in Southeast Asia (cf. Myrdal, 1968). Moreover, in terms of the problem of the formation of an international community, relationships among the units of East and Southeast Asia become very important.

Comparative study should not be hindered by "region-parochialism." It should proceed to broader typologies and generalization, as a sequel to the identification of regional problems and the accumulation of regional data.

Chapter 8
Patterns of Nation-Building in Asia

I n Chapter 7, I have attempted to elucidate the factors responsible for "successful" modern nation-building in Japan in contrast to the belated and fruitless efforts in Korea. While the course of nation-building in the countries was vastly different, Japan and Korea had several predisposing factors in common. They both were characterized by a high degree of ethnic and linguistic homogeneity; they both had to some extent absorbed Confucian values and governing techniques; and yet they both could point to an indigenous political unity which preceded this cultural borrowing.

A variety of explanations have been offered to account for the differences in the nation-building experiences of these two countries. Marxists tend to focus on the development and control of the means of production. They suggest that while the seeds of a modern (*i.e.*, capitalistic) system of production were visible during the Yi dynasty (1392–1910), the natural growth process was distorted by the intrusion of the West and, later, by the external manifestations of Japan's rapid economic development. In contrast, Japan's successful industrialization and attainment of sustained economic growth after 1868 was possible *because* production forces had grown sufficiently during the Edo period (1603–1868) to provide the necessary foundation. This interpretation, then, focuses attention on the different levels of production achieved in Edo Japan and the late Yi dynasty in Korea.

Another explanation contrasts Korea's proximity to a major cultural center with Japan's relative isolation. An island country, separated from the continent by rough seas, Japan never experienced invasion or military conquest by China, and so Chinese cultural influence was always subjected to certain limitations.

126

Thus, the Japanese were in a position to exercise some degree of selectivity. This meant that indigenous cultural elements could be more easily preserved. This explains in part the ability of Shinto—Japan's native religion—to survive into modern times despite the intrusion of Buddhism and Confucianism. In the Edo period, Confucianism was promoted by the ruling warrior-aristocracy both as a justification for their monopoly of political power and as a source of governing techniques. As a result, Confucianism achieved a position of dominance in the Edo period Partly in response to this development, a movement began in the mid-Edo period to resuscitate native traditions, and men like Motoori Norinaga (1730–1801) and Hirata Atsutane (1776–1843) directed their efforts toward the revival of early Japanese literature. They succeeded in focusing considerable attention on these neglected Japanese classics and, in the process, gave them a level of sophistication that had often been lacking. This movement was known as *Kokugaku*, or School of National Learning, and was designed to challenge the predominance of *Jugaku*, or Confucian Studies. The appearence of such a movement at this time was not without significance for the political changes after 1868, which saw a return of the emperor to the center of the stage, for after all the figure of the emperor was at the very heart of these native traditions.

In Korea, while the Koryŏ dynasty was essentially a Buddhist regime, the long-lived Yi dynasty was very much a Confucian state on the Chinese model. Confucianism was the official state doctrine; unlike Japan, where a military aristocracy ruled perpetuated by heredity, in Korea Confucianism was effectively promoted and maintained by a civil service examinations system, whereby a knowledge of Confucian texts was the key to social mobility and political status. Thus it would seem that Korea's physical proximity to the continent resulted in a more complete absorption of Chinese values and institutions. Of course, we cannot ignore the appearance of a new school of practical learning during the late Yi dynasty, which was essentially an indigenous response to the challenges of the modern world. However, since this was still basically a school of Confucianism, it is hardly comparable to the Japanese situation where native trends were preserved and ultimately revived and channeled into the modern nation-building effort. In this connection, the significance of Japan's geographic location at the periphery of the Chinese cultural sphere cannot be overlooked.[1]

While both of the above approaches have elements to recommend them, I focused on two somewhat different points in the previous chapter. In the first place, I stressed the importance of linkages *between* the center and the periphery within a given country, and the impact this might have on the nation's ability to channel its native resources into the nation-building process. For example, as Henderson (1968) has pointed out, the high degree of centralization found during the Yi dynasty, coupled with the existing social homogeneity, resulted in a structural vacuum between the political center—Seoul—and the periphery—the villages and the countryside. This supports my contention that if political linkages between the center and the periphery are lacking, the fruits of political centralization and social homogeneity cannot be effectively channeled into the nation-building process.

In Japan, such links were there, having grown out of the tension between centralizing and decentralizing forces which had been so artfully combined by the Tokugawa rulers to give their *baku-han* system its unique character. While the *shōgun* was a national leader to whom all other feudal lords (*daimyō*) were linked by oaths of allegiance, his direct authority did not penetrate into the various feudal domains of which Japan was composed at this time. Thus, while a precedent for loyalties to be focused on a single national leader was established, there remained sufficient local autonomy to generate growth and change at the local level. Hence, by the end of the Edo period Japan had some degree of urbanization (as a result of the growth of castle towns), a system of local production which was linked to a nationwide distribution network, as well as other patterns valuable for establishing nationwide transportation and communication systems, and the like. This meant that Japan had the mechanics—the structural linkages —necessary to effectively channel traditional elements into the

[1] Stein Rokkan (1973, p. 90–91) notes an extremely important similarity between East Asia and Europe. He writes: "The great paradox of Western Europe was that it developed a number of strong centers of territorial control at the edge of an old Empire; the decisive thrusts of state formation and nation-building took place on the peripheries of the political vacuum left by the disruption of the old Roman Empire. To this extent, there is a tantalizing similarity with the Far East: China, the imperial center; centripetal Korea, the Asian counterpart to France; the seaward periphery Japan, the equivalent of 'off-shore island' England."

process of building a modern nation. So, after 1868, the new government was able to skillfully reorder certain key ingredients in the political system and create the family state in which all authority ultimately resided in the emperor and was transmitted orderly to the countryside through traditional village institutions and, of course, the patriarchal family system.

The dark side of this success story, however, is well known. While reliance on traditional values and institutions made rapid nation-building possible, it exerted an unhealthy influence on the final product. Japan had to pay a steep price in the form of the anachronistic Imperial state of the 1930s. It took a disastrous defeat in World War II to generate the kind of fundamental changes in the social system which enabled Japan to move in the direction of establishing civil liberties and social equality, and to experience a high degree of popular participation and secularization in the political realm.[2] Of course, these internal consequences of Japan's distorted growth process had external manifestations as well. Japan annexed Korea in 1910, became deeply involved in Manchuria, and ultimately intervened directly in China in the 1930s. This suggests an additional observation: what is good for one unit in a region may have disastrous consequences for the other units in the same region.[3]

Southeast Asian Cases

Moving from East Asia to Southeast Asia, one is struck by the kaleidoscopic nature of the rise and fall of empires and kingdoms

[2] Japan and Germany are similar in this respect. Bendix (1969, pp. 251–52) argues that "both countries industrialized successfully. Both were characterized by a symbiosis between tradition and modernity that was tension-ridden but enduring. In both cases this symbiosis was subjected for a considerable time to the cumulative impact of the 'industrial arts' and the 'process of rationalization'. . . . Yet the most drastic social and political change of both countries has *not* occurred as a result of that slow adaptation to the matter-of-fact outlook of modern technology which Veblen extrapolated from the English experience. In both countries, the mainstays of social and political tradition in the midst of modernity have been destroyed by conquest, military occupation, and partition."

[3] Again the Japanese and German cases are parallel. This suggests the necessity of synthesizing the theory of political development with that of the international system. In other words, we have to take into consideration both the input from the international system and the output to it, and try to develop theory which can deal with the interrelationship between national and international development.

in this area. To date, no sociologist or political scientist with the necessary command of the historical background of this region has come forth to supply us with models and theories of premodern nation-building in Southeast Asia. Even in Eisenstadt's *The Political Systems of Empires*, which covers a vast area and a lengthy time span, the historical kingdoms and empires of Southeast Asia such as Srivijaya, Angkor, Malacca, Sumatra, and Java are given no attention. Thus the pioneering work in this field remains to be done.

However, even a superficial comparison of East and Southeast Asia makes clear a number of dissimilarities. In the first place, East Asia is historically a culturally uniform region. In contrast to this, Southeast Asia was repeatedly subjected to penetration from two cultural centers, India and China. Benda (1969) proposed that Southeast Asia be classified into three subregions according to the dominant cultural influence—*i.e.*, into Sinicized, Hinduized, and (since the Philippines had been relatively isolated from outside influences until the arrival of the Spaniards) Hispanized regions. Of course, with the arrival of the Muslims and the spread of Islam after the fourteenth century, we must add a fourth, Islamized, superimposed over about half of the Hinduized subregion. Obviously, this sort of highly differentiated historical environment not only affected premodern nation-building, but made a lasting imprint still in evidence today. Moreover, I hold that the considerable intraregional variation in Southeast Asia is an important factor accounting for the disparity in nation-building experiences between East and Southeast Asia. Much has been made of the role of value systems in providing a motivational basis for industrialization. With this view in mind, we can identify four main types of value systems operating in Southeast Asia (corresponding to the four subregions identified above): a Chinese, a Filipino, a Hinayana Buddhist, and a Hindu-Islamic. At this level of abstraction, the value systems found in East Asia can be lumped into a single category, so that there is hardly a comparable degree of intraregional variation in the two areas.

In the second place, while the East Asian states may be classified as agrarian societies, in Southeast Asia a number of societies organized around trade and merchant activities appeared alongside the inland, agrarian-type societies. Therefore, in any analysis of nation-building in Southeast Asia, we would have to take into consideration the distinction between these two types of society.

In the third place, in contrast to the pattern of social homogeneity found in East Asia, Southeast Asian countries—especially Singapore, Malaysia, and Thailand—are often classified as "plural societies." A common feature of these societies is the existence of a large overseas Chinese community which is integrated to a considerable extent into the host society, but without loss of ethnic consciousness and solidarity. Although 800,000 Koreans presently reside in Japan, the Chinese number only 50,000 (25,000 in Korea), and so here again the pattern in East Asia diverges from that found in Southeast Asia. The idea of "consociational democracy" (Daalder, 1971) has recently attracted much attention. It presents a challenging hypothesis which should be tested in the Southeast Asian setting. In such an undertaking, however, several points must be kept in mind. What is the significance of preexisting conditions favorable to pluralism and tolerance? This issue emerges in a comparison of Lijphart's work (1969) with Daalder's. On the one hand, Lijphart stresses the importance of conscious efforts by elites to build up a "consociational nation" and thereby offset the destabilizing effects of cultural fragmentation. On the other hand, Daalder, drawing primarily on the Dutch and Swiss experiences, underlines the role of predisposing factors which seem favorable to pluralism and tolerance. So I would suggest that in order to deal effectively with the Southeast Asian case, we must determine to what extent, if any, factors favorable to pluralism and tolerance were present.

The first point to keep in mind if we are to apply the notion of consociational nations to Southeast Asia is the problem of functional imbalances along ethnic lines in heterogeneous societies. The pattern in Southeast Asia is for the Chinese communities to play a dominant role in trade and commercial activities. This problem can be expressed diagramatically. Figure 8.1 shows a consociational nation in which a consociational unified elite is leading (left side) and groups A and B are performing all functions in society evenly (right side). Figure 8.2 shows unbalanced performance of functions by groups of different ethnic origins. This amounts to a functional division of labor based on ethnic origin in which different goods are distributed by different groups—*i.e.,*

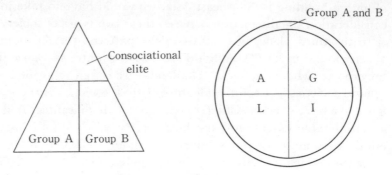

Fig. 8.1.   Consociational nation

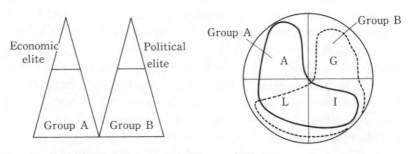

Fig. 8.2.   Precariously balanced nation

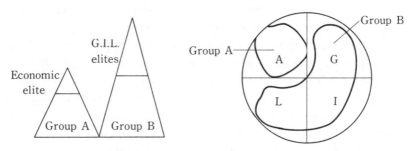

Fig. 8.3.   Alienated nation

Notes: 1) For A.G.I.L., see Parsons (1956).
         2) A = adaptation (economy), G = goal-attainment (politics), I = integ-
            ration, L = latency (maintenance of patterns of values).

political goods are distributed to group B through its political elites, while economic goods are distributed throughout group A by its economic elite. In this fashion, a compensatory equilibrium is maintained. An example of this kind of compensatory equilibrium can be found in pre-1966 Nigeria when the Ibo dominated the business function while the Hausa monopolized key political positions. We can see from the Nigerian case how unstable this compensatory equilibrium setup tends to be. Figure 8.3 represents the most unbalanced situation. Here, group B dominates not only the political aspect but also the integrative and "latency" aspects such as religion, language, and education. Hence the position of group A is really that of a minority group rather than that of an equal partner in a consociational nation. However, group A is predominant in the economic realm, and since it is a well-known sociological law that people seek status congruency, this is potentially an explosive situation. Incidents in Malaysia in 1969 attest to this fact. Therefore, when we talk about conscious efforts by elites to achieve consociation, we must be aware of the problems presented by these kinds of functional imbalances and of the precarious nature of the compensatory equilibrium approach.

A second point that must be brought up when considering Southeast Asia is one made by Daalder concerning the international environment. Specifically, we must ask if Southeast Asian nations are likely to be as fortunate as the Netherlands and Switzerland in having an international environment conducive to undertaking the time-consuming process of building a consociational nation. In this connection, the attitude of the People's Republic of China is a crucial variable to keep in mind, for it not only is a major power center in Asia, but also presumably could greatly influence the behavior of the Chinese communities throughout the area.

A third factor to be dealt with is the impact of Western imperialism on Southeast Asian countries. Although Thailand was spared this experience, all other Southeast Asian societies underwent varying degrees of social and cultural disruption as a direct result of policies initiated by the colonizing countries. An extreme case is the example of the Philippines, where Spanish rule resulted in residual "feudalizing" effects (Benda, 1969, p. 37), whose vestiges are still visible today. In this connection, it might be useful to compare the Philippines with the countries of Latin America. Nevertheless, among Southeast Asian nations it is also important to distinguish between the type of colonial rule (*i.e.,* direct or indirect) experienced. In those areas where indirect rule was practiced, indigenous social and political continuity were far better preserved than in areas under direct rule. In this context, the following observation by Benda (1969, p. 37) is worthy of note: "The 'Oriental despotisms' " in "directly ruled areas—as in Burma, Java and Cochinchina, for example—were almost invariably replaced by Western-style administrations manned by Europeans. Education in such areas benefitted a sociologically far more heterogenous—if numerically no less restricted—clientele, with the result that the nascent modernizing elites in 'directly' administered regions tended to be less tied to the precolonial social and political status-quo, and hence less conservative."

A fourth and final point concerns Japan's international behavior following its rapid nation-building experience, specifically the impact this behavior had on Japan's neighbors, China and Korea. Korea had been under Japanese rule since 1910, but after Japan's full-scale aggression on the continent got underway in the 1930s, this rule became especially repressive. Proscription of the Korean language to the extent of forcing Koreans to render their names according to the Japanese pronunciation was but one example of the extreme form the Japanese will to subjugate the Koreans took. In addition, efforts were made to impose the Shinto religion on the Korean people by building shrines and forcing people to visit them and pay homage. Large numbers of workers were ruthlessly forced into labor battalions and moved around at will to replace Japanese manpower in occupied areas. Policies such as these not only caused social disruption in Korea, but resulted in a deeply rooted animosity on the part of Korean people toward their Japanese mentors. Hence the Korean nation-building efforts after 1945— in both North and the South—have shared a common base: a commitment to eradicating all vestiges of Japanese influence. Both the founder of the Democratic People's Republic in North Korea, Kim Il Sung, and the founder of the Republic of Korea in the South, the late Syngman Rhee, were former leaders of the resistance movement. Even today, a shadow of animosity lingers, and relations between Japan and Korea are accordingly somewhat delicate.

A related issue, that of the Japanese occupation of Southeast Asia between 1941 and 1945, has yet to be adequately researched. In Singapore and Malaysia the Chinese communities suffered heavily, and the occupation continues to be a source of bitterness for them. Although Japan's occupation of Southeast Asia was part of its overall war effort, and as such was characterized by intolerance and ruthlessness of the sort seen in Korea, it did trigger a fundamental change in the international environment of Southeast Asia by bringing an end to Western colonialism in that region.[4] In Benda's (1969, pp. 40–44) study, the impact of Japanese occupation on the internal political and social structure of these nations was examined in the context of the type of colonial rule to which they were subjected. His thesis is that in areas where indirect rule prevailed, the impact of Japan's occupation was superficial. Therefore, postwar nation-building programs were carried out by elites who had continuity with the prewar period. In contrast to this, where colonial rule had been direct, such as in Burma and Java, the collapse of the colonial government resulted in a vacuum, and ultimately in the reordering of the elite structure. Benda (1969, pp. 42–43) calls attention to the fact that "since the peasantry's acquiesence in, if not support for, wartime policies was doubtless one of the most crucial Japanese targets, their efforts to win allies among religious leaders followed logically from a realistic understanding of the key role of *pong yi* and *ulama* (and perhaps also of the lower Catholic clergy) in peasant life. . . . In stark contrast to the colonial powers' aloofness vis-à-vis Southeast Asian religions, the Japanese apparently fostered religious leaders together in mass movements under military or naval control. . . . On the whole, the Japanese apparently utilized, revolutionized, and consolidated the religious elites and thus endowed them with potential strength—vis-à-vis both traditional and nationalist elites—unprecedented in modern Southeast Asian history." While I am not qualified to comment on this at present, in view of Japan's total religious insensitivity and general intolerance in Korea, I must confess that I am skeptical. On the other hand, however, it does seem probable, in view of the agrarian/nativist element in Japanese militarism, that Japanese occupation encouraged or at least tolerated religious movements among the

---

[4] Japan offers a fascinating case study in the effects of military occupation, which I have attempted to develop in another paper written in Japanese (Watanuki, 1973).

peasants. In any event, this is something to be spelled out more clearly in subsequent research.

For Further Comparison

What I have discussed above is not nation-building *per se*, but factors—especially historical factors—which circumscribe, but do not wholly determine, modern nation-building efforts. It can easily be argued that since human actions never take place in a vacuum, and hence are always subject to influences arising from an existing context, we must focus on these historical factors in order to gain meaningful insights into what actually went on. However, we cannot ignore the fact that there is often a wide area of choice as to the form the human element—*i.e.*, the human management of nation-building efforts—can take. We can see this clearly in the postwar nation-building efforts of the two Koreas. Sharing common historical antecedents, these two nations approached the tasks associated with modern nation-building, such as penetration, integration, participation, and economic growth, in quite divergent manners. Today, these two countries are challenging each other with their accomplishments. In a similar context, we can note that China and the Democratic Republic of Vietnam have put forth their approach to nation-building for the world to see as a viable alternative.

There is an implication for the strategy of comparative research on modern nation-building to be drawn from this. It is not necessarily advantageous to be limited to intraregional comparisons. For example, North Korea's approach to nation-building has more in common with North Vietnam's than with South Korea's. Moreover, as we saw earlier, in order to isolate a single historical factor, such as the legacy of Spanish colonial rule, the Philippines could be most effectively compared with Latin American nations. This same strategy could be applied to other factors such as the effects of indirect or direct colonial rule (*i.e.*, a comparison of some Southeast Asian and African nations), the size and function of "mini" states (*i.e.*, a comparison of Singapore and Malta), and others.

Chapter 9
Japanese Attitudes toward the Rest of the World

The data and analysis presented in this chapter deal with the perceptions and ideas of Japanese concerning international society. In other words, we have sought to probe Japanese attitudes toward all phenomena located outside the geographic, racial, cultural, political, and economic entity "Japan." Like all attitudes, they include cognitive, emotional, and evaluative components, are arranged in a fairly stable attitudinal structure, and are susceptible to systematic observation. I attempted to tap these attitudes by analyzing responses to a survey on international attitudes.

The attitudes treated here—international attitudes—are directed toward phenomena which are remote from the daily lives of most people (in comparison, for example, with school issues or commodity prices). International phenomena are multifarious, and in many cases ordinary citizens do not possess adequate background to allow the standard attitudinal sequence of cognition, emotion, and evaluation to take place. This is evident in those extreme cases in which the majority of respondents fall in the "don't know" or "no answer" categories. Furthermore, international attitudes tend to be inconsistent, and a follow-up survey would likely reveal some instability over time.

Because of the special characteristics of international attitudes, we designed the theoretical framework of the study[1] and chose the

[1] The field work was carried out by the *Chūō chōsasha* (Central Survey Research Center). 1. Survey universe: All Japanese men and women over 15 years of age, excepting those resident in Okinawa; 2. Planned sample: 4,000 persons; 3. Sampling method: stratified, two-stage, random sampling; 4. Survey method: interview with questionnaire; 5. Survey period: May 29 through June 5, 1972; 6. Completed interviews: 3,304 (82.6 percent); 7. Incomplete interviews: 696; 8. Reasons for incompletion: respondent moved (100), extended absence (109), short absence (283), residence unclear (43), respondent refused (139), other (22).

questions which comprise it with the following objectives in mind:

1. to examine the consistency, direction, and intensity of reactions to a wide variety of international phenomena;

2. to discriminate as clearly as possible among cognition, emotion, and evaluation as attitudinal components;

3. to collect sufficient data to piece together a more or less complete view of the contemporary Japanese attitude structure. Most of the thirty-three questions were designed to discover the diverse objects of Japanese international attitudes and to measure reactions to them. In the future, we intend to subject the resultant attitudinal clusters to multivariate analysis;

4. to identify the factors which underlie these international attitude clusters. In other words, we will search for clusters of independent and intervening variables which determine the dependent variables, international attitudes. The types of independent variable clusters which affect international attitudes have been fairly clearly delineated by previous research: they include age (or generation), education level, and socioeconomic status. In this study, age has been emphasized, with secondary attention to education level and socioeconomic status.

As intervening variable clusters, we have used political orientation and conception of human nature (*ningenkan*). In graphic form, the relationship between these variable clusters can be portrayed as follows:

Independent variable	Intervening variable	Dependent variable
Age (generation)	Political orientation	
Education level	Conception of	International attitudes
Socioeconomic status	human nature	

The subjects of the thirty-three questions asked, and the attitude clusters they concern, are as follows:

Q1 Level of interest in international affairs (strength of cognitive drive)

Q2, 3 Relative interest in certain geographic areas (attitudinal intensity by area)

Q4 Nations thought to be trustworthy (evaluation)

Q5 Nations constituting a threat (evaluation)

Q6 Nations liked (emotion)

Q7 Nations disliked (emotion)

Q8a, b, c, d, e View of international politics (cognition, evaluation)

Q9 Japan's relations with the U.S.A., China, and the Soviet Union (cognition, evaluation)

Q10 The Sino-Japanese War (cognition, evaluation)

Q11 Postwar Japan-China relations (cognition, evaluation)

Q12 Normalization of Sino-Japanese relations (cognition, evaluation)

Q13 Policies for normalization (cognition, evaluation)

Q14 Relations with Korea (cognition, evaluation)

Q15 Future changes in U.S.-Japan relations

Q16 Conflict of economic interests between Japan and the U.S. (cognition, evaluation)

Q17 Japan-Soviet relations (cognition, evaluation)

Q18 Geographic limits of Asia (cognition)

Q19 Japan's cultural and social status (cognition)

Q20 Significance of the Pacific War (cognition, evaluation)

Q21 Aid to Asian nations (evaluation)

Q22 Nature of aid (cognition, evaluation)

Q23 Threat perception (cognition)

Q23SQ Threat content (cognition)

Q24 Measures to insure Japan's security (cognition, evaluation)

Q25 Okinawan base problem (cognition, evaluation)

Q26 Nuclear armament for Japan (evaluation)

Q27 Familiarity with other peoples (evaluation, emotion)

Q28 Trust of other peoples (evaluation)

Age and International Attitudes

The universe of this survey was composed of both men and women over 15 years of age, and 3,304 interviews made up the sample. When the age distribution of these respondents is compared with that of the survey universe as a whole, it is evident that the interviewed samples include slightly fewer respondents in the 20–24 and over-60 age groups, but this did not cause any serious distortion. Several occupational characteristics of the sample should be noted, however. The very high proportion of students in the 15–19 age group reflects the tremendous increase in the percentage of persons attending high schools and colleges in the last few years. The precipitous decrease since 1955 of the percentage of Japan's population engaged in agriculture is reflected in the very small proportion of respondents under 35 who are employed in agriculture. In the 18–30 age bracket, the percentage of respondents in white-collar, sales, or service occupations is remarkably high.

Table 9.1:   Party preference by age (in percentages)

	LDP	JSP	Kōmeitō	DSP	JCP	None,* D.K.	
15–17	9.8	9.3	2.0	1.5	2.5	75.0	(N = 204)
18–19	13.5	11.3	2.3	0.8	0.8	71.4	(N = 133)
20–24	17.1	15.3	3.6	3.9	3.9	58.5	(N = 386)
25–29	20.8	15.9	3.8	3.0	3.0	50.8	(N = 370)
30–34	26.3	23.8	4.3	1.5	1.5	39.1	(N = 400)
35–39	30.2	22.7	4.2	1.0	1.0	36.9	(N = 401)
40–44	33.8	21.7	3.2	1.6	1.6	36.0	(N = 314)
45–49	36.3	14.2	4.6	1.7	1.7	39.6	(N = 240)
50–59	43.2	14.5	4.1	0.2	0.2	34.0	(N = 442)
Over 60	46.9	8.5	1.7	0.5	0.5	40.6	(N = 414)

*Including "Other"

Next, let's look at political orientation broken down by age group (Table 9.1). In terms of political party support, 70 percent of those under 20 years of age claimed "no party support" or answered "don't know" (D.K.);[2] for those between 20 and 30, this figure was 50 percent. The average among all respondents was "other"— 0.3 percent, "no party support"—38.7 percent, and "don't know" —6.2 percent. In other words, for those in their teens and twenties, political inclinations have not, by and large, coalesced into solid support for a particular political party. Moreover, the level of exposure to political information proves to be relatively low for those

---

[2] This low level of party support among people under 20 is confirmed by other surveys. A July 1971 survey, for example, showed that 67.1 percent of the 16–19-year-olds questioned supported no party, and 8.8 percent answered "don't know" (Kōmei Senkyo Renmei, 1972, p. 72).

Table 9.2:   Views on the present Constitution by age (in percentages)

	Revise according to national sentiment	No revision whatso- ever	Neither	D.K.	
15–19	20.2	51.0	13.1	15.7	(N = 337)
20–29	22.1	41.1	18.8	18.0	(N = 756)
30–39	22.0	39.1	17.5	21.5	(N = 801)
40–49	20.0	36.3	18.6	25.1	(N = 554)
50–59	22.4	33.5	18.6	25.6	(N = 442)
Over 60	21.0	22.0	14.0	43.0	(N = 414)

in their teens and twenties, progressively greater for those in their thirties, forties, and fifties, and again low for those in their sixties.[3]

Nevertheless, it would be a mistake to draw the conclusion that the young are depoliticized. In order to determine reactions to the fundamental principles on which the postwar political and social systems are based, we asked the respondents to evaluate the post-war Constitution (Table 9.2) and the emperor system. The responses of those 29 and under show convincingly that, compared with other age groups, the young are indeed heirs of the predominant postwar value system. "Don't know" answers were relatively few.

What kind of international attitudes do the various age groups of respondents, particularly the young, display?

1. Interest in international affairs, revealed in terms of desire for information, follows a reverse-U-type curve across age brackets in much the same way as political and social participation, activity, and consciousness: interest among people in their forties and fifties is higher than that in other age groups. In contrast, it is interesting that questions such as Q3, which asked about the sense of being "related" to various areas and nations, revealed that younger people feel related to more areas and nations. However, all age groups with the exception of the over-60's showed a high degree of sense of relatedness to events in Vietnam; in this case the young were not particularly outstanding. Overall, the total sense of relatedness of the under-20 group was great, due

[3] This reverse-U-shaped curve appears often with regard to social participation, awareness and activity levels, organizational membership, and such political activities as voting and participation in election campaigns.

not to concentration on any one nation or area but rather to a tendency to name a larger variety of areas—such as Korea, Southeast Asia, Eastern Europe, and so on—as related to themselves personally.

Table 9.3: "Liked" countries by age (in percentages)

	U.S.A.	W. Eur.	China	Other countries	None	Other,* D.K.	
15–19	8.3	49.3	4.2	10.7	16.0	16.6	(N = 337)
20–24	10.9	35.2	2.1	9.9	26.9	28.2	(N = 386)
25–29	11.4	31.9	3.0	6.1	26.5	27.3	(N = 370)
30–39	11.6	28.0	2.2	6.4	29.5	30.9	(N = 801)
40–49	15.3	20.2	2.5	6.6	26.9	28.5	(N = 554)
50–59	14.0	14.3	5.2	6.8	34.4	35.9	(N = 442)
Over 60	15.7	8.2	1.9	4.1	26.8	29.0	(N = 414)

*Including "Like all"

Table 9.4: "Disliked" countries by age (in percentages)

	U.S.A.	U.S.S.R.	China	Other countries	None	Other,* D.K.	
15–17	14.7	11.8	4.9	17.7	33.3	17.7	(N = 204)
18–19	21.8	11.3	8.3	7.4	33.8	16.5	(N = 133)
20–24	12.2	12.2	6.0	10.8	41.2	17.6	(N = 386)
25–29	7.8	12.2	4.9	12.5	36.8	25.9	(N = 370)
30–39	7.5	12.9	4.2	9.3	39.1	26.9	(N = 801)
40–49	5.4	21.5	3.2	6.7	34.7	28.5	(N = 554)
50–59	4.3	26.0	4.5	6.3	31.9	27.1	(N = 442)
Over 60	3.4	21.5	2.4	3.0	29.7	39.8	(N = 414)

*Including "Dislike all"

2. Levels of threat perception, trust, like and dislike, and feelings of familiarity toward other nationalities also vary by age group. "Don't know" answers increase with age: the 15–19 age group gave the fewest "don't know" answers. A tendency to reject the United States in favor of Western Europe is apparent in lower age groups. Favorable attitudes toward Western Europe among young people are particularly evident along the emotional dimension of "like-dislike" (see Tables 9.3 and 9.4), and rejection of the United States is clearly revealed in both the emotional ("dislike") and the evaluative ("threat") dimensions. The United States occupies first place among "threatening" countries chosen by members of the 15–24 age group, and seems to be the most

"disliked" nation for the 15–19 age group. Of course this standing is only relative, and it should be noted that a large percentage of young people answered in an optimistic manner that they do not feel threatened by any country. Furthermore, percentages were also fairly high for both the Soviet Union and China, and it would hence be a mistake to tar young people indiscriminately with the brush of anti-American nationalism. Nevertheless, the contrast between these figures and the responses of more mature respondents who trust the United States and perceive the Soviet Union as threatening is particularly striking.

It is significant that the young seem to reject the United States in favor of Western Europe rather than other Asian nations. An exception to this tendency appears in answers relating to "trusted" countries: 19.3 percent of people in their twenties (more than in any other age group) said they trust Asian people.

3. Relatively few respondents in lower age groups answered "don't know" to questions concerning Japan's position among the great powers, and so the overall pattern of responses is quite clear (Table 9.5). Consistent with the rejection of the United States mentioned above, a fairly large number of youths would approve a shift in diplomatic emphasis from the United States to the Soviet Union and China; particularly with regard to the Soviet Union, it is evident that young people show relatively little dissatisfaction over Soviet failure to return the northern territories seized at the end of World War II (roughly one-fourth in the teen-age and twenties age groups are dissatisfied). Those desiring closer relations with the Soviet Union in the future numbered 40.7 percent of those 15–19, and 35 percent of those in their twenties

Table 9.5:   Japan's future direction vis-à-vis the U.S.A., U.S.S.R., and China by age (in percentages)

	Stay close to U.S.A.	Harmony with China	Harmony with U.S.S.R.	Other	D.K.	
15–19	19.0	39.2	10.4	5.9	25.5	(N = 337)
20–29	22.4	35.6	6.2	6.9	29.0	(N = 756)
30–39	22.1	37.8	3.7	5.6	30.7	(N = 801)
40–49	24.2	35.6	3.2	6.3	30.7	(N = 554)
50–59	28.1	31.9	2.0	6.3	31.7	(N = 442)
Over 60	26.3	22.0	1.7	3.6	46.4	(N = 414)

(the overall average for all age groups was 28.4 percent). Regarding relations with the U.S., 35.6 percent of the 15–19 group feel that relations will continue as before (the average for all age-groups was 42.7 percent), and 33.5 percent feel that relations will get worse (overall average 23.4 percent). Hence the young are more pessimistic than average concerning the future of U.S.-Japan relations.

With regard to Japan-China relations, a consistent pattern of responses according to age group appears. A high percentage of those in the over-60 group passively answered "don't know," while those in the under-20 group were generally very decisive. For those in between, the pattern is not rectilinear but refracted according to generational experience. With regard to the Sino-Japanese War, for example, many of those in their twenties answered "other," indicating that their interpretations go beyond the simple solutions offered in the survey, while those in their forties and fifties, who experienced the Sino-Japanese War in their youth, answered clearly with very few "don't know" responses.

4. A clear, rectilinear relationship according to age group appears with regard to perception of threats to Japan's independence and security, the nature of the threats, measures to insure Japan's security, bases in post-reversion Okinawa, and nuclear armament. Perception of external threats to Japan's security is comparatively widespread among young people, and most feel that the threat of involvement in war resulting from Japanese cooperation with American policy is most dangerous. As for measures to insure Japan's security, young people most often choose idealistic alternatives such as "should call upon other nations to respect Japan's position," and "other nations should be called upon to respect Japan's unarmed, peaceful status." Most young people show strong dissatisfaction with the continued existence of American bases on Okinawa after its reversion to Japanese ownership, and they adamantly oppose nuclear armament. In this sense, those in the 15–29 age group are the direct heirs of Japan's postwar pacifism and "nuclear allergy" (Table 9.6).

5. Young people generally named a relatively large number of Asian nations, and Vietnam was often included by respondents in the 15–24 age group (Table 9.7). With regard to Japan's social and cultural similarity to other nations (Table 9.8), however, a

Table 9.6:   Nuclear armament by Japan by age (in percentages)

	Should arm immediately	Will arm in future	Should never arm	Other, D.K.	
15–19	0.9	30.5	74.8	3.9	(N = 337)
20–29	2.2	20.0	68.5	9.2	(N = 756)
30–39	0.9	21.8	65.5	11.7	(N = 801)
40–49	1.4	23.8	63.2	11.6	(N = 554)
50–59	2.3	26.5	57.0	14.3	(N = 442)
Over 60	2.4	20.8	51.4	25.4	(N = 414)

Table 9.7:   Naming Asian nations by age

	Named at least one	D.K.	Average number named	
15–17	95.6%	4.4%	9.2	(N = 204)
18–19	92.5	7.5	8.6	(N = 133)
20–24	91.2	8.8	8.7	(N = 386)
25–29	88.6	11.4	7.6	(N = 370)
30–39	87.4	12.6	7.2	(N = 801)
40–49	83.8	16.2	7.8	(N = 554)
50–59	86.2	13.8	6.5	(N = 442)
Over 60	69.8	31.2	6.4	(N = 414)

Table 9.8:   Social and cultural similarity to Japan by age (in percentages)

	Asia	U.S.A./ W. Eur.	Neither	Other	D.K.	
15–19	21.1	63.2	5.6	0.9	9.2	(N = 337)
20–29	20.2	59.7	8.9	0.7	10.6	(N = 756)
30–39	23.2	51.2	9.1	1.4	15.1	(N = 801)
40–49	22.4	48.6	7.8	1.1	20.2	(N = 554)
50–59	25.1	41.2	9.3	0.5	24.0	(N = 442)
Over 60	21.5	31.9	8.2	0.2	38.2	(N = 414)

majority responded that Japan is closest to the United States and Western Europe, and a very small number answered "don't know." Objectively, it can be argued that this view is, in fact, accurate, and there certainly is no reason to quarrel with or regret this perception. There is definitely a favorable attitude toward Western Europe among the young, but this does not necessarily imply that they are turning their backs on Asia.

Evaluations of the Pacific War, however, reveal some confusion in the 15–29 age group. If the over-60 age group which regularly has a high rate of "don't know" answers is excluded, it is remarkable that over 30 percent of the responses concerning the Pacific War from the 15–19 age group as well as those 20–29 group fall in the "don't know" and "irrelevant to me" categories. This is surprising, since the young generally show a high degree of awareness of international events, but it is understandable since they did not actually experience the war. Perhaps it is fair to assume that the younger generation in other Asian nations would answer in the same manner. Nevertheless, to the extent that young Japanese must deal with the older generation of Asians that suffered directly from the war, this evaluative gap can be expected to become a source of friction.

Those respondents in their forties and fifties who actually experienced the Pacific War in their youth gave the lowest percentage of "don't know" answers. When responses are calculated including only those who responded in some manner other than "don't know" or "irrelevant to me," it is easy to see the difference in the attitudes of the 15–19, 30–49, and over-50 age groups. But even here, it is apparent that those aged 15–24 who did not experience the war are heirs to the evaluative tendencies revealed by those in their thirties and forties.

Finally, concerning Japanese aid to other Asian nations, it is striking how high a percentage of "don't know" answers are given by those in the over-60 bracket. In this age group, of course, are many who have never become accustomed to the concept of aiding developing countries, and to some extent their reticence may be due to a feeling that domestic welfare programs for the aged should come before foreign aid. Even so, relatively few show direct disapproval. Most of those in the 15–29 age brackets, however, take a positive attitude toward aid, and are generous about conditions. Relatively few answered "don't know."

Educational Level and International Perception

Both in Japan and elsewhere a difference in educational level often brings with it significant differences in many sociopolitical attitudes. In Japan's case, the spread of higher education has been amazing in recent years. During the 1960s, the proportion of 18–22-year-olds enrolled in universities and colleges jumped from 10 to 20 percent and has continued to grow to the level of 40 percent by 1975. Senior high school education, in which 75 percent of the 15–17-year-olds were enrolled as of 1972, will reach a kind of saturation point of 90 percent by 1980.

The most conspicuous result of a higher educational level is the increased articulateness in responses to questions. Especially in the responses to such remote problems as those concerning the international environment, those with low educational levels often fail to respond at all. In our data, on a number of questions, the proportion of "don't know" and "not ascertained" responses among those with nine years of schooling or less was as high as 40 or even 50 percent; in contrast, in their answers to the same questions, those with college educations gave only 20 to 30 percent "don't know" or "not ascertained" responses. The correlation between the educational level and the degree of articulation and crystallization of opinions concerning remote international matters is a universal phenomenon, which has been observed in other countries too (cf. Almond, 1950, p. 127).

Another frequent finding both in Japan and elsewhere is that the higher their educational level the more liberal people become in their views on various sociopolitical issues. However, a fairly wide range of variation exists in this respect from society to society, for historical and other reasons. In the case of the United States, liberalism of educated people is manifested in their opinions concerning such domestic issues as civil liberties and racial problems, but often it does not have much to do with their opinions on international problems.[4] However, in Japan's case, liberalism is closely connected with the postwar democracy based on the principles of the present Constitution. Our data clearly show higher commitment to the present Constitution among those with college educations (Table 9.9), 60 percent of whom want no revision of the present Constitution (in comparison with 28 percent of grade school graduates). The same tendency is found in the

---

[4] Regarding civil liberties issues, see Stouffer (1955). Concerning ethnic minority problems, see, for example, Louis Harris and Associates (1971, pp. 220, 225). However, on such international issues as the Vietnam War, those with college educations were found to be rather hawkish (Rosenberg, Verba, and Converse, 1970, pp. 54–59; Louis Harris and Associates, 1971, pp. 85, 112, 114).

Table 9.9:   Views on the present Constitution by educational level
(in percentages)

	Revise according to national sentiment	No hasty revision	Neither	D.K., N.A.	
Low	19.4	27.7	18.5	34.3	(N = 1,430)
Middle	24.5	40.0	17.2	18.2	(N = 1,301)
High	21.8	60.7	12.6	5.0	(N = 262)

Table 9.10:   Views on the emperor by educational level (in percentages)

	Should participate more actively in politics	Should gradually get rid of the emperor system	Neither	D.K., N.A.	
Low	19.4	27.7	18.5	34.3	(N = 1,430)
Middle	24.5	40.0	17.2	18.2	(N = 1,301)
High	21.8	60.7	12.6	5.0	(N = 262)

Table 9.11:   Measures to insure Japan's security by educational level
(in percentages)

	Autonomous defense by JSDF	Strengthen JSDF but rely on security treaty	Decrease JSDF and ask for understanding	Unarmed nation	New autonomous system	Other	D.K., N.A.	
Low	13.1	17.3	14.8	14.0	3.1	1.7	36.1	(N = 1,430)
Middle	10.3	17.7	23.3	20.8	4.3	1.8	21.9	(N = 1,301)
High	12.2	22.9	24.4	25.6	5.3	2.7	6.9	(N = 262)

Table 9.12:   Japan's future direction vis-à-vis the U.S.A., U.S.S.R., and
China by educational level (in percentages)

	Stay close to U.S.A.	Harmony with China	Harmony with U.S.S.R.	Other	D.K., N.A.	
Low	24.8	25.0	3.2	4.9	42.2	(N = 1,430)
Middle	24.0	39.7	4.1	6.2	26.1	(N = 1,301)
High	22.9	51.1	5.0	9.9	11.1	(N = 262)

Table 9.13: Nuclear armament by Japan by educational level (in percentages)

	Should arm im- mediately	Will arm in future	Should never arm	D.K., N.A., other	
Low	2.0	20.0	59.0	19.0	(N = 1,430)
Middle	1.2	23.7	66.8	8.3	(N = 1,301)
High	1.9	29.0	64.9	4.2	(N = 262)

response to the question concerning the position of the emperor (Table 9.10), in which 60 percent of the college-educated people wanted to see the gradual waning of the emperor system.

Moreover, a significantly different pattern from that found in the U.S. is that, in Japan's case, educational level is correlated with certain attitudes concerning foreign and defense issues such as non-armament, neutralism, and even pacifism. Actually this is a rather natural corollary of the commitment of those with a higher education to the present Constitution, which contains the famous Article 9 forbidding Japan to wage war. As is shown in Table 9.11, a plurality of those with college educations prefer to decrease or even to abolish the Self-Defense Forces (JSDF). They feel deep anxiety about Japan's security under the present Japan-U.S. Security Treaty and would like to see Japan move closer to China (Table 9.12).

However, in the response to the question on nuclear arma-ment, the differences among educational groups are much smaller (Table 9.13). There are two possible explanations for this. On the one hand, we can point to the universal prevalence of anti-nuclear feeling among the Japanese people regardless of level of education, due to the historic experiences of Hiroshima and Nagasaki. On the other hand, a "realistic" opinion that "Japan might arm itself with nuclear weapons in the future" is held more widely among highly educated persons, which does not necessarily contradict a commitment to not possessing nuclear weapons at present, but does leave open a wider field of choice for the future.

With respect to feelings of like and dislike, familiarity, trust, and threat concerning other peoples and nations, there are considera-ble variations according to educational level. As we have seen, these feelings often contradict each other; or perhaps we should say that they are ambivalent. As we look at the breakdown by educational levels, we find that contradictions and ambivalence rather increase in the highly educated group. For example, asked about their familiarity with various peoples, 40 percent of those with college educations answer that they feel most familiarity with Asian peoples, in comparison with 35 percent of those with high school educations and 25 percent of those with grade school educations. In their feelings of trust toward various peoples, those with college educations show more trust toward Asian peoples than do those of lower educational levels. And increased aid to Asian nations gets overwhelming support among those with higher educations. However, in terms of "liked" countries, the more educated they are, the more the respondents are attracted by Western European countries (Table 9.14). When they are asked about sociocultural similarities between Japan and other countries, their educational level clearly correlates with their recognition of similarities between Japan and Western countries rather than those between Japan and other Asian countries. Sixty-eight percent of those with college educations see Japan as having more sociocultural similarity with Western European countries or the United States than with other Asian countries.

The position of China in this context seems to call itself to our attention. As we have seen, those with college educations prefer

Table 9.14: "Liked" countries by educational level (in percentages)

	U.S.A.	W. Eur.	China	Other Asian countries	None	Others, all, D.K., N.A.	
Low	12.3	14.0	2.8	4.1	29.9	36.9	(N = 1,430)
Middle	12.8	32.4	3.2	3.0	26.7	21.8	(N = 1,301)
High	16.8	32.4	1.5	2.7	28.6	17.9	(N = 262)

Table 9.15: "Disliked" countries by educational level (in percentages)

	U.S.A.	U.S.S.R.	China	Other	None	Other,* D.K., N.A.	
Low	4.3	17.3	3.4	6.2	33.3	35.4	(N = 1,430)
Middle	8.5	17.6	5.0	9.5	36.7	22.7	(N = 1,301)
High	11.5	19.1	3.1	11.4	44.3	10.7	(N = 262)

*"Dislike all"

a foreign policy of moving toward an equidistant relationship between the United States and China. However, on the levels of like and trust, those people show very little difference from other educational groups. Those with college educations do not seem to be more attracted emotionally by China. Rather, they see China as a possible threat. In other words, their reasoning goes: China is a threat; therefore we need to pay more attention to it and to try to develop a closer relationship with it. I would like to argue that this is a sign of the emergence of realistic attitudes, that those with college educations tend to refuse to view other countries in such emotional terms as "trust" or "dislike" (Table 9.15). In response to a question about disliked countries, the answer "none" (as distinguished from "don't know" and "not ascertained") increases in frequency with the educational level of respondents.

So far we have examined only two variables, age and education, and their correlations with international attitudes. Because the spread of higher education in Japan has been continuous since before World War II and has accelerated during the postwar period, especially in the last decade, age and educational levels are cor-

Table 9.16: Views on the emperor by age and educational level (in percentages)

Age	Educ.	Should participate more actively in politics	Should gradually get rid of the emperor system	Neither	D.K., N.A.	
20–24	L	18.5	27.2	30.9	23.5	(N = 81)
	M	11.6	31.9	39.8	16.7	(N = 216)
	H	9.5	47.6	38.1	4.8	(N = 42)
	S*	2.2	64.4	28.9	4.4	(N = 45)
25–29	L	26.9	16.7	29.5	26.9	(N = 383)
	M	18.1	21.9	39.7	20.2	(N = 657)
	H	14.3	37.3	39.7	8.7	(N = 126)
40–59	L	30.5	10.1	35.3	24.1	(N = 606)
	M	26.0	17.0	42.6	14.4	(N = 312)
	H	22.1	26.0	45.5	6.5	(N = 77)
Over 60	L	31.5	8.1	23.7	36.6	(N = 333)
	M	49.1	9.1	32.7	9.1	(N = 55)
	H	35.3	11.8	41.2	11.8	(N = 17)

*Student

related with each other. Younger age groups contain a higher ratio of those with high school or college educations, and the highly educated group is biased toward youth in its age composition. Therefore, we have to distinguish the causal effect of age from that of education and to investigate the attitudinal characteristics of subgroups based on the combination of age and education.

On several issues, such as the present Constitution, the emperor system, measures to insure Japan's security, and social and cultural similarity to Japan, we can see typical examples of mutual reinforcement by age and education, where both age and education are working as independent factors in the same direction. The case of views on the emperor system is shown in Table 9.16, in which age and education working together cause the highest ratio of anti-emperor system opinion among young and highly educated people (48 percent in the group 20–24 years old with college educations) and the lowest among those who are old, poorly educated (8 percent among those over 60 years old with grade school educations). In similar ways, young age and high education contribute to the support for the present Constitution, to the perception of Japan as more similar to Western Europe and the U.S.A. than to Asian countries, and to the choice of unarmed neutrality.

The second type of correlation between age, education, and international attitudes is that in which age and education are working in different directions, resulting in a rather dispersed distribution of attitudinal characteristics among various age-education groups. An example of this is the response to the question about "most familiar peoples." As we can see from the data, the education factor is contributing to increasing the feeling of familiarity to Asians, but in the perceived level of familiarity to Europeans among those who are in their early twenties there is no variation by educational level. In this case, the causal factor is age, not education.

The third type is a spurious correlation between age and international attitudes with the educational factor as the real determinant. The "aid to Asian countries" question is an example of this. There seemed to be some correlation between age and the opinion favoring increased aid to Asian countries. However, when we broke down the data further by educational level, the correlation between age and opinion disappeared. Thus, the factor determining attitudes toward foreign aid is educational level; but it remains true that we find more young people than old people favoring foreign aid among our respondents.

Thus we can say, based on the above cited data, that domestic liberalism and international pacifism and neutralism will continue or even grow steadily in Japan, since they are enhanced by both age and education. There are also signs of growing internationalism as expressed by attitudes such as those favoring increases in foreign aid which seem to be correlated with higher education. However, there are also some signs of an increasing identity crisis. The more educated people are, the more they feel a familiarity with Asian peoples on one hand; but on the other, they recognize the greater similarity of their society to Western European and American ones than to other Asian societies.

Partisanship and International Attitudes

In spite of an increasing tendency toward nonpartisanship and electoral independence, about 70 percent of the Japanese electorate, when asked in polls, still mention the name of a party they support. And it has been empirically proven that the party support thus ascertained has a high correlation with voting behavior and other political orientations.[5]

Among the correlations between party support and political orientations, the highest is that between party support and self-definition as politically "conservative" or "progressive (*kakushin*)," with the result that Liberal Democratic Party supporters are heavily on the conservative side, Democratic Socialist and Kōmei supporters in the middle, and Japan Socialist Party and Japan Communist Party supporters on the progressive side. Next to this, opinions concerning the present Constitution and the emperor system are highly correlated with party support. To many, the present Constitution has been the symbol of postwar democracy,

---

[5] The majority of a candidate's support comes from supporters of the party with which the candidate is affiliated. However, for the narrow margin which divides the winner from the loser in many contests, votes from nonpartisans or even the small number of votes from defected supporters of other parties are vital.

which liberated Socialists and Communists from suppression by the state. Therefore it is no wonder that JSP and JCP supporters favor the present Constitution. Or, to put it the other way around, perhaps those people who favor the present Constitution have been attracted by the JSP or the JCP because of the activities of those parties in defending the present Constitution against the moves by the right wing of the LDP. However, the correlation with party support is more conspicuous in the evaluation of the emperor system than in the evaluation of the Constitution (Table 9.17). Attachment to the emperor system is clustered with preferences for other prewar traditional values such as those emphasizing conformity and an authoritarian family system (Watanuki, 1967). Therefore, we can still see the existence of cultural politics, in which the value cleavage of tradition and modernity is superimposed on the political cleavage of conservative and progressive and, furthermore, related to party alignments of Right (LDP), middle (DSP and Kōmei), and Left (JSP and JCP). Thus, in Japan's case, domestic issues such as education, which touch on values, have often aroused generalized confrontation between the LDP and other parties, because they stimulate a whole cluster of partisan, conservative and progressive, feelings among not only political leaders but also ordinary citizens.

Where do foreign policy divisions lie? In contrast with the United States where the correlation between party identification and opinions on foreign policies is quite thin, in Japan's case, the relationship between party support and opinions on foreign policies has been fairly clear throughout the postwar period (Mendel,

Table 9.17: Views on the emperor by party support (in percentages)

	Should participate more actively in politics	Should gradually get rid of the emperor system	Neither	N.A. D.K.,	
LDP	35.5	12.7	34.2	17.6	(N = 985)
DSP	14.3	25.2	45.4	15.1	(N = 119)
Kōmei	26.1	23.5	32.2	18.3	(N = 115)
JSP	24.1	31.0	32.5	12.4	(N = 539)
JCP	7.4	51.9	25.9	14.8	(N = 54)

1961, pp. 247–48). There are several reasons why this has been so. First of all, we can mention inexperience in bipartisan or multipartisan foreign policy formation. The continued dominance of the Liberal Democratic Party in the Diet has made it unnecessary to seek support from the opposition parties through compromises. On the other hand, the opposition parties have tended to be extremely severe in their criticisms of LDP foreign policy because they have been totally alienated from foreign policy making. The opposition parties—especially the JSP and the JCP, and in recent years the Kōmei Party also—often have organized mass protest actions outside the Diet against the government's foreign policy. In the second place, Japan's defense policy has a peculiar problem in the constitutional status of the Self-Defense Forces; since the constitutional problem has been symbolically linked with a whole set of political orientations and values, a defense issue can easily become a diffuse and emotional confrontation between the LDP and opposition parties and can facilitate the crystallization, polarization, and party-relatedness of opinions even among ordinary citizens (Converse and Dupeux, 1962).

Responses to our survey question on defense policy are shown in Table 9.18. The first thing which attracts our attention is the relatively low ratio of those in the D.K. and N.A. category (less than 30 percent). The level of crystallization of opinions on this kind of problem seems to be relatively high. Second, the rank order of percentages of the supporters of each party favoring alternative measures neatly coincides with other rank orders such as Right-Left, conservative-progressive, disapproval-approval of the

Table 9.18:   Measures to insure Japan's security by party support
(in percentages)

	Increase JSDF & security treaty	Decrease or abolish JSDF & depend on goodwill	Creation of new defense system	Other, D.K., N.A.	
LDP	46.1	28.4	3.2	22.2	(N = 985)
DSP	42.1	40.3	4.2	13.5	(N = 119)
Kōmei	23.5	45.3	6.1	25.2	(N = 115)
JSP	18.9	56.2	4.6	20.2	(N = 539)
JCP	9.3	61.1	9.3	20.4	(N = 54)

present Constituiton and of the emperor system, except for some minor exceptions. The position of the DSP supporters is one such exception. When we compare Tables 9.17 and 9.18, we notice an oscillation of the position of the DSP supporters in the rank order of parties. In their opinions on defense policy, DSP supporters are close to LDP supporters, while relatively fewer DSP supporters favor the revival of the emperor system, thus indicating their politically conservative but socially less traditional character. Another minor exception is the low percentage of JCP supporters favoring "creation of a new defense system." The Communist Party has said that it will dissolve the present JSDF after it successfully takes over the government, and then create an entirely new people's army. Only 9 percent of JCP supporters favor such a step at the present moment, but this is quite understandable, since the JCP does not talk much about the future build-up of a new army but is extremely vocal about the dissolution of JSDF as its short-range target.

Japan's relationship with China has also been a hot partisan issue. Although opinions favoring the improvement of the relationship "as fast as possible" have been dominant, the real issue has been whether that sort of improvement should be made in spite of the danger of impairing the U.S.-Japan relationship. In actual fact, after this survey was completed, the normalization of Sino-Japanese relations was achieved by the Tanaka government, partly stimulated by the improvement in U.S.-China relations. However, since it is still uncertain whether this happy Japan-China-U.S. triangle can be maintained or not, it will be worthwhile to look at the result of a question asking respondents to choose which relationship—that with the United States, China, or the U.S.S.R.—is more important to Japan. We have to be very cautious in interpreting this finding, since this is a forced choice. The low percentage of those who chose the Soviet Union does not mean that the Japanese populace has no desire to improve the relationship between Japan and the Soviet Union. As a matter of fact, in answer to other questions asking about the necessity of that relationship, a plurality of the populace said it considers the relationship to be necessary. However, two things should be mentioned in connection with the Russo-Japanese relationship. First, even in the minds of JCP supporters, China carries an overwhelming

Table 9.19: Future of Japan-Soviet relations by party support (in percentages)

	Should improve	Improve but dissatisfied with non-return of northern territory	Need not improve relations	Other	D.K., N.A.	
LDP	24.2	36.8	9.8	2.4	26.8	(N = 985)
DSP	38.7	40.3	6.7	0.8	13.4	(N = 119)
Kōmei	27.8	26.1	7.8	2.6	35.7	(N = 115)
JSP	35.6	31.9	4.3	3.5	24.7	(N = 539)
JCP	40.7	31.5	7.4	1.9	18.5	(N = 54)

Table 9.20: Threatening nations by party support (in percentages)

	U.S.A.	W. Eur.	U.S.S.R.	China	Other	None	All, D.K., N.A.	
LDP	7.7	0.5	33.5	15.1	2.1	11.5	29.5	(N = 985)
DSP	16.0	1.7	26.9	22.7	5.0	7.6	20.1	(N = 119)
Kōmei	12.2	—	25.2	11.3	2.6	10.4	38.2	(N = 115)
JSP	22.4	0.6	22.4	10.4	3.5	11.5	29.2	(N = 539)
JCP	51.9	—	7.4	11.1	1.9	9.3	18.6	(N = 54)

Table 9.21: "Liked" countries by party support (in percentages)

	U.S.A.	W. Eur.	China	Other	None	All, D.K., N.A.	
LDP	19.1	21.9	2.4	7.0	26.4	23.0	(N = 985)
DSP	23.5	31.9	5.0	7.6	22.7	9.2	(N = 119)
Kōmei	6.1	20.0	4.3	10.4	26.1	33.0	(N = 115)
JSP	9.6	30.8	5.6	9.8	25.6	18.5	(N = 539)
JCP	1.9	33.3	13.0	20.5*	22.2	9.3	(N = 54)

*Including 5.6 percent liking U.S.S.R.

weight, in spite of the fact that the JCP has been in dispute with the Chinese Communist Party. Second, in comparison with supporters of other parties, JCP supporters seem to favor improvement of the relationship with the Soviets more, but the difference is not impressive. We can see this even more clearly in Table 9.19, which shows that more than 30 percent of JCP supporters expressed dissatisfaction with the Soviet Union's refusal on the problem of the reversion to Japan of the northern islands of Habomai, Shikotan, and two others in the Kuriles.

In views and feelings on nations and peoples also, there are considerable variations according to party support. Partisan perceptions of "threatening nations" are shown in Table 9.20; LDP supporters are at one extreme and JCP supporters at the other. A plurality of JCP supporters see the United States as the most threatening nation to Japan, and very few feel a threat from the Soviet Union's external behavior; although they may not particularly like the Soviet Union (see Table 9.21), but at least they think that the Soviet Union is no threat to Japan.

Comparing Table 9.20 with the breakdown of responses to the same question by educational level, we find one interesting contrast. Concerning the perception of a Chinese threat, the educational level produced a clear difference. In contrast, concerning the perception of threats from the United States and the Soviet Union, not educational level but partisanship counts most.

In terms of liked nations, partisanship is again linked very closely to differences in liking the United States. An interesting phenomenon in Table 9.21 is that JCP supporters seem to be more attracted by Western European countries than supporters of other parties. The same tendency is manifested in their view on the sociocultural position of Japan in the world: JCP supporters tend to regard Japan as close to Western Europe and the United States socially and culturally.

As a matter of fact, it is not difficult to interpret these phenomena. From a Marxist analytical viewpoint, Japan is a highly developed capitalist country like Western European and North American societies. Moreover, the strategy of revolution which the JCP has been pursuing under the leadership of Chairman Miyamoto Kenji is that of "revolution in advanced countries," the models for which are neither the Soviet nor the Chinese Communist Parties, but the Italian and French Communist Parties.[6] Therefore, it is no wonder that JCP supporters view Japanese society as closer to Western European or American societies.

[6] In July 1972, as one of the activities celebrating the fiftieth anniversary of its founding, the Japan Communist Party organized an international theoretical conference, the central themes of which were "problems of revolutionary movements in highly developed capitalist countries" and "united front and government based on it." Participants included delegates from the communist parties in Australia, West Germany, France, Great Britain, Italy, Spain, and Japan, and an observer from the United States. For the proceedings of this conference, see Japan Communist Party (1972).

One more interesting point concerning JCP supporters is that they are not very concerned with aid to Asian countries. JCP supporters are more critical of increased aid to Asian countries than are the supporters of other parties. Again this is understandable because the JCP says very little about the aid problem, but when it does speak about it, it criticizes aid by capitalist countries, including Japan, as "neo-colonialism."[7]

What conclusions can be drawn from the preceding analysis? It is apparent that the international attitudes of ordinary citizens, regardless of their party affiliations, do not determine the foreign policies of the government. And the voting behavior of the electorate is not determined primarily by the voters' international attitudes nor by appeals made to them during a campaign, even when foreign policy is an election issue.

However, the relatively high degree of crystallization, party-relatedness, and value-relatedness of international attitudes described and analyzed above can provide some insights into Japanese foreign policy making and suggestions about how to approach it. First of all, when the opinions of the rank and file show such party-relatedness, activists and leaders can be expected to be more explicitly party-related in their opinions on a broad range of international issues, reinforced by their perceptions that their followers are party-related in their attitudes. Second, the leaders of the opposition parties pick up on issues not only because of their own value related political orientation but also because of their perception of their followers and their expectation of a dramatic effect. A good recent example was the emperor's visit to the United States. In this case, the JCP, and later the JSP as well, skillfully linked a diplomatic protocol problem to a whole set of political orientations and values, arguing that the emperor's visit to the United States would have the far-reaching sociopolitical effect of turning Japan in a conservative and traditional direction.

Whether the LDP leaders were simply thoughtless or whether

[7] Certainly the Japan Communist Party does not fail to discuss "economic and technological cooperation between Japan and Asian countries" as a subitem in its explanation of foreign policy. However, the content of this item is very abstract, as shown by the following sentence: "Based on the principle of international solidarity aiming at social progress, and as a highly developed industrial power, [a Japanese government based on a democratic coalition] will actively promote economic and technological cooperation, in order to contribute to world peace, independence of peoples, and the social progress of all mankind" (Japan Communist Party, 1973).

they had in mind the result which the opposition leaders claimed in initiating the emperor's visit to the United States is not certain. What seems clear is that American decision-makers lacked sufficient knowledge concerning political dynamics and values in Japan to effectively handle this and other problems of the U.S.-Japan relationship.

International attitudes of the general public in any country have been suspect for their volatility with good reason. In an open and democratic society, however volatile they may be, at least they function as a constraint—whether to be respected or to be manipulated—to the foreign policy decision-makers. Moreover, with the increase of nongovernmental transnational activities such as tourism, studying abroad, sister-city relationships, and multinational corporations, international attitudes and behavior of the general public of each nation have increased their impact on international relations. As such, the author hopes, the picture presented in this chapter of the Japanese perception of the rest of the world can serve to enhance mutual understanding between Japan and other nations.

References

Abegglen, James C. *The Japanese Factory: Aspects of Its Social Organization.* Glencoe, Ill.: The Free Press, 1958.

Allison, Graham. "Conceptual Models and the Cuban Missile Crisis." *American Political Science Review*, September 1969 (Vol. 63, no. 3).

Almond, Gabriel. *The American People and Foreign Policy.* New York: Harcourt, Brace & Co., 1950.

Arora, Satish K. "Participation and Nation-Building." Paper presented to the Asian Working Party on State and Nation-Building, Singapore, November 22–25, 1971.

Benda, Harry J. "The Structure of Southeast Asian History: Some Preliminary Observations." In R. O. Tilman (Ed.) *Man, State and Society in Contemporary Southeast Asia.* New York: Praeger, 1969.

Bendix, Reinhard. *Nation-Building and Citizenship.* New York: Wiley, 1964; Doubleday, Anchor Books, 1969.

Collings, Randall. "A Comparative Approach to Political Sociology." In R. Bendix (Ed.) *State and Society: A Reader in Comparative Political Sociology.* Boston: Little, Brown, 1968.

Converse, Philip, and Dupeux, George. "Politicization of the Electorate in France and the U.S." *Public Opinion Quarterly*, Spring 1962 (Vol. 26, No. 1.)

Coser, Lewis A. *Men of Ideas: A Sociologist's View.* New York: The Free Press, 1965.

Curtis, Gerald L. *Election Campaigning Japanese Style.* New York: Columbia University Press, 1971.

Daalder, Hans. "On Building Consociational Nations: The Cases of the Netherlands and Switzerland." *International Social Science Journal*, 1971 (Vol. 23, No. 3).

Dahl, Robert A. *Polyarchy: Participation and Opposition.* New Haven, Conn.: Yale University Press, 1971.

Dore, R. P. *Land Reform in Japan.* London: Routledge & Kegan Paul, 1959.

Duverger, Maurice. *Political Parties.* London: Methuen, 1964.

Eberhard, Wolfram. "Problems of Historical Sociology." In R. Bendix (Ed.) *State and Society: A Reader in Comparative Political Sociology.* Boston: Little, Brown, 1968.

Eisenstadt, S. N. *Modernization: Protest and Change.* Englewood Cliffs, N. J.: Prentice-Hall, 1966.

Flanigan, William H. *Political Behavior of the American Electorate.* Boston: Allyn & Bacon, 1968.

Fukutake Tadashi, *Nihon nōson shakairon.* Tokyo: University of Tokyo Press, 1964. Published in English as *Japanese Rural Society* by Oxford University Press, 1967.

Fukutake Tadashi. "Social Character of the Village Community." In *Man and Society in Japan.* Tokyo: University of Tokyo Press, 1962, pp. 78–101.

161

Galenson, Walter. *Trade Union Democracy in Western Europe*. Berkeley and Los Angeles, Calif.: University of California Press, 1961.

Hani Gorō. *Tōyō ni okeru shihonshugi no keisei* (Formation of Capitalism in Asia). Tokyo: San'ichi shobō, 1948.

Henderson, Gregory. *Korea: The Politics of the Vortex*. Cambridge, Mass.: Harvard University Press, 1968.

Hofstadter, Richard. "Pseudo-Conservatism Revisited: A Postscript—1962." In Daniel Bell (Ed.) *Radical Right*. New York: Doubleday, 1963.

Holt, Robert T. and Turner, John E. *The Political Basis of Economic Development*. Princeton, N.J.: Van Nostrand, 1966.

Ikeuchi Hajime (Ed.). *Shimin ishiki no kenkyū* (Studies in Civic Attitudes). Tokyo: University of Tokyo Press, 1974.

Inglehart, Ronald. "The Silent Revolution in Europe: Intergenerational Change in Postindustrial Society." *American Political Science Review*, December 1971 (Vol. 65, No. 4).

Inoue Mitsusada. *Nihon kokka no kigen* (The Origin of the Japanese State). Tokyo: Iwanami shoten, 1960.

Institute of Statistical Mathematics, Ministry of Education. *Kokuminsei no kenkyū* (A Study of Japanese National Character). Tokyo: Shiseidō, 1961.

Institute of Statistical Mathematics, Ministry of Education. *A Study of the Japanese National Character: The Fifth Nationwide Survey*. Research Report General Series No. 38, 1974.

Ishida, Takeshi. "The Development of Interest Groups and the Pattern of Political Modernization in Japan." In R. E. Ward (Ed.) *Political Development of Modern Japan*. Princeton, N.J.: Princeton University Press, 1968.

Japan Communist Party. "Shūgiin senkyo deno sōten to Nihon kyōsantō no godai kihon seisaku" (Issues in the General Election and Five Basic Policies of the Japan Communist Party.) *Zen'ei* (Vanguard), February 1973, No. 351.

Japan Communist Party. *Zen'ei*, August 1972, No. 342, pp. 184–342.

Kawano Kenji. *Furansu kakumei to Meiji ishin* (The French Revolution and the Meiji Restoration). Tokyo: Nippon Hōsō Shuppan Kyōkai, 1961.

Keizai Shingikai Kokuminsenkōdo Chōsa Iinkai. "Kokumin senkōdo chōsa—daiichiji shūkei kekkahōkoku" (Preliminary report on the preference of the people). 1972.

Kim, Jae-on. "Path Analysis and Causal Inference." Memorandum to CPSPC Participants, October 1969.

Kōmei Senkyo Renmei. *Dai nanakai tōitsuchihōsenkyo to yūkensha* (The Seventh Unified Local Elections and the Voter), II. 1972.

Kōmei Senkyo Renmei. *Sangiin tsūjōsenkyo no jittai* (A Survey Report on Ordinary Elections for the House of Councillors). 1974.

Kōmei Senkyo Renmei (Ed.) *Seiji ishiki ni kansuru chōsa hōkokusho* (Report on Political Attitudes Survey). March 1972.

Kornhauser, William. *The Politics of Mass Society*. Glencoe, Ill.: The Free Press, 1959.

Kuwabara Takeo (Ed.) *Burujowa kakumei no hikaku kenkyū* (A Comparative Study in Bourgeois Revolutions). Tokyo: Chikuma shobō, 1964.

Kyogoku, J., and Ike, N. "Urban-Rural Differences in Voting Behavior in Postwar Japan." *Proceedings of the Department of Social Sciences, College of General Education, University of Tokyo*, 1959, (No. 9).

Langdon, Frank. *Politics in Japan*. Boston: Little, Brown, 1967.

La Palombara, Joseph. *The Italian Labor Movement: Problems and Prospects*. Ithaca, N. Y.: Cornell University Press, 1957.

Laponce, J. A. *Government of the Fifth Republic*. Berkeley and Los Angeles, Calif.: University of California Press, 1961.

Lazarsfeld, P. F; Barton, A; and Lipset, S. M. "The Psychology of Voting." In G. Lindzey (Ed.) *Handbook of Social Psychology*, Vol. 1. Cambridge, Mass.: Addison-Wesley, 1954.

Lee, Chong-sik. *The Politics of Korean Nationalism*. Berkeley and Los Angeles, Calif.: University of California Press, 1963.

Lee, Hahn-been. *Korea: Time, Change, and Administration*. Honolulu: East-West Center Press, 1968.

Lee, Young Ho. "Kankoku no seijifūdo to minshushugi" (Korean Political Culture and Democracy). *Kankoku Jiji*, October 1971 (No. 60).

Lee, Young Ho. "Social Change and Political Participation in Korea." Paper presented at the Conference on Tradition and Change in Korea, Seoul, September 1-6, 1969.

Levy, Marion J., Jr. "Contrasting Factors in the Modernization of China and Japan." In S. Kuznets, W. E. Moore, and J. J. Spengler (Eds.) *Economic Growth: Brazil, India, Japan*. Durham, N. C.: Duke University Press, 1955.

Lijphart, Arend. "Consociational Democracy." *World Politics*, January 1969 (Vol. 21, no. 2).

Linebarger, Paul M. A; Chu, Djang; and Burks, Ardath W. *Far Eastern Government and Politics: China and Japan*. Princeton, N. J.: Van Nostrand, 1967.

Lipset, S. M. *Political Man*. New York: Doubleday, 1960; Doubleday Anchor, 1963.

Lipset, S. M. "Socialism: Left and Right—East and West." *Confluence*, Summer 1958 (Vol. 7, No. 2).

Lockwood, David. *The Blackcoated Worker*. London: Allen & Unwin, 1958.

Louis Harris and Associates. *The Harris Survey Yearbook of Public Opinion 1970*. New York: Louis Harris and Associates, 1971.

Maruyama, Masao. *Thought and Behavior in Japanese Politics*. Oxford: Oxford University Press, 1963.

Masamura Kimihiro; Nakamura Shūichirō; and Iida Tsuneo. *Gendai Nihon keizaishi* (Economic History of Post–World War II Japan). Tokyo: Chikuma shobō, 1976.

Massey, Joseph A. *Youth and Politics in Japan*. Lexington, Mass.: D. C. Heath, 1976.

Matsumoto, Yoshiharu Scott. "Contemporary Japan: The Individual and the Group." *Transactions of the American Philosophical Society*, New Series, 50, Part I, 1960.

Mendel, Douglas H., Jr. *The Japanese People and Foreign Policy.* Berkeley and Los Angeles, Calif.: University of California Press, 1961.

Ministry of Labor (Japan) Daijin Kambō Rōdō Tōkei Chōsa-bu. *Kinrōsha seikatsu ishiki chōsa hōkoku* (A Survey on Workers' Attitudes toward their Lives). December 1971.

Moore, Barrington, Jr. *Social Origins of Dictatorship and Democracy.* Boston: Beacon Press, 1966.

Myrdal, Gunnar. *Asian Drama*, Vol. I. New York: Pantheon, 1968.

Nakane Chie. *Tateshakai no ningenkankei.* Tokyo: Kōdansha, 1967. Published in English as *Japanese Society* by University of California Press, 1972.

Nelson, Joan. "The Urban Poor: Disruption or Political Integration in Third World Cities." *World Politics*, March 1970 (Vol. 22, no. 3).

Nie, Norman; Powell, G. Bingham, Jr.; and Prewitt, Kenneth. "Social Structure and Political Participation: Developmental Relationships, I and II." *American Political Science Review*, June, September 1969 (Vol. 63, nos. 2, 3).

Nihon Shakaigakkai Chōsa-iinkai (Ed.). *Nihon shakai no kaisōteki kōzō* (The Stratification of Japanese Society). Tokyo: Yūhikaku, 1958.

Nikkei Business Henshūbu. *Nippon no kigyō kankyō* (Japan's Business Environment). Tokyo: Nihon keizai shimbun, 1974.

OECD. *Review of National Policies for Education: Japan.* Paris: OECD, 1971.

Ōkubo, Sadayoshi. *Rōdō no miraiyosoku* (Prediction of Future Labor Trends). Tokyo: Teikoku chihōgyōsei gakkai, 1972.

Parsons, Talcott. *Economy and Society.* London: Routledge and Kegan Paul, 1956.

Passin, Herbert. "The Sources of Protest in Japan." *American Political Science Review*, June 1962 (Vol. 56, No. 2), p. 393.

Pye, Lucian W. "The Non-Western Political Process." *Journal of Politics*, August 1958 (Vol. 20, no. 3).

Rekishigaku Kenkyūkai (Research Association of Historical Science). *Meiji ishin kenkyūshi kōza* (A Series on the History of Research on the Meiji Restoration). Tokyo: Heibonsha, 1958; new supplementary volume, 1969.

Rokkan, Stein. "Cities, States, and Nations: A Dimensional Model for the Study of Constraints in Development." In S. Rokkan and S. N. Eisenstadt (Eds.) *Building States and Nations.* Beverly Hills, Calif.: Sage Publications, 1973.

Rokkan, Stein. "The Mobilization of the Periphery." In Stein Rokkan, *Citizens, Elections, Parties.* New York: David McKay Co., 1970.

Rokkan, Stein. "Models and Methods in the Comparative Study of Nation-Building." *Acta Sociologica*, 1969 (Vol. 12, No. 2).

Rosenau, James N. *Public Opinion and Foreign Policy.* New York: Random House, 1961.

Rosenberg, Milton J.; Verba, Sidney; and Converse, Philip. *Vietnam and the Silent Majority.* New York: Harper & Row, 1970.

Rustow, Dankwart. *The Politics of Compromise: A Study of Parties and Cabinet Government in Sweden.* Princeton, N. J.: Princeton University Press, 1955.

Rustow, Dankwart. "Scandinavia: Working Multiparty Systems." In S. Neumann (Ed.) *Modern Political Parties*. Chicago, Ill.: University of Chicago Press, 1956.

Sakamoto, Yoshiyuki. "A Study of the Japanese National Character: The Fifth Nationwide Survey." *Annals of the Institute of Statistical Mathematics*, Supplement 8, 1974.

Scalapino, Robert A., and Masumi, Junnosuke. *Parties and Politics in Contemporary Japan*. Berkeley and Los Angeles, Calif.: University of California Press, 1962.

Scott, James C. "Patron-Client Politics and Political Change in Southeast Asia." *American Political Science Review*, March 1972 (Vol. 66, No. 1).

Shikauchi Nobutaka. "Nihon no masukomi no genjō to Fuji-Sankei gurūpu no chōsen" (Japanese Mass Communications and the Challenge of the Fuji-Sankei Group). *Seiron*, September 1974.

Shinohara Hajime and Matsushita Keiichi. "Nihon Shakaitō no shisō jōkyō" (The State of Thought in the Japan Socialist Party). *Chūō kōron*, December 1962.

Shinohara Hajime and Miyazaki Ryūji. "Sengo kaikaku to seiji karucha" (Postwar Reforms and Political Culture). Tokyo Daigaku Shakaikagaku Kenkyūjo (Ed.) *Sengo kaikaku 1: Kadai to shikaku* (Postwar Reforms I: Problems and Perspectives). Tokyo: University of Tokyo Press, 1974.

Steiner, Kurt. "Popular Political Participation and Political Development in Japan: The Rural Level." In R. E. Ward (Ed.) *Political Development in Modern Japan*. Princeton, N. J.: Princeton University Press, 1968.

Stouffer, Samuel A. *Communism, Conformity and Civil Liberties*. New York: Doubleday, 1955.

Tanaka Yasumasa. "Toward a Multi-level, Multi-stage Model of Modernization: A Case Study of Japanese Opinion Leaders on the Present and Future National" Goals. *Gakushuin Review of Law and Politics*, 1974 (Vol. 9).

Tawara Kōtarō. *Hadaka no Nihon Kyōsantō* (The Japan Communist Party Unmasked). Tokyo: Nisshinhōdō shuppanbu, 1972.

Thayer, Nathaniel B. *How the Conservatives Rule Japan*. Princeton, N. J.: Princeton University Press, 1969.

Tōyama Shigeki; Imai Seiichi; and Fujiwara Akira. *Shōwa shi* (A History of the Shōwa Era). Tokyo: Iwanami shoten, 1955.

Tsuji, Kiyoaki. "Decision-Making in the Japanese Government: A Study of Ringisei." In R. E. Ward (Ed.) *Political Development in Modern Japan*. Princeton, N. J.: Princeton University Press 1968.

Tsuji Kiyoaki. "Shizenteki handō to seijiteki handō" (Natural Reaction and Political Reaction). *Sekai*, January 1952.

Ueyama Shumpei. *Meiji ishin no bunseki shiten* (A Framework for the Analysis of the Meiji Restoration). Tokyo: Kōdansha, 1968.

Verba, Sidney; Ahmed, Bashiruddin; and Bhatt, Anil. *Caste. Race and Politics*. Beverley Hills, Calif.: Sage Publications, 1971.

Verba, Sidney, and Nie, Norman H. *Participation in America*. New York: Harper & Row, 1972.

Verba, Sidney; Nie, Norman H.; and Kim Jae-on. *The Modes of Democratic Par-*

ticipation: A Cross-National Comparison. Beverley Hills, Calif.: Sage Publications, 1971.

Verba, Sidney, Nie, Norman H. and Kim Jae-on. *Political and Social Stratification: A Cross-National Comparison.* Forthcoming.

Ward, Robert E. (Ed.) *Political Development in Modern Japan.* Princeton, N. J.: Princeton University Press, 1968.

Ward, Robert E., and Rustow, Dankwart A. (Eds.) *Political Modernization in Japan and Turkey.* Princeton, N. J.: Princeton University Press, 1964.

Watanuki, Joji. "Amerika ni yoru Nihon minshuka" (Democratization of Japan by the United States). Jōchi Daigaku Kokusaikankei Kenkyūjo, Chōsa to Shiryō, 1973 (No. 3).

Watanuki, Joji. "Political Attitudes of the Japanese People." *The Sociological Review Monograph,* 1966 (No. 10).

Watanuki, Joji. "Social Sciences in Japan." *International Social Sciences Journal,* 1975 (Vol. 27, No. 1).

Watanuki, Joji. *Tokyo tomin no seiji ishiki to tōhyō kōdō: Senkyō chōsa kiyō 1967 No. 3* (Political Attitudes and Voting Behavior of the Tokyo Electorate: Monograph Electoral Survey Series). Tokyo: Kōmei Senkyo Renmei, 1967.

White, James W. *The Sōkagakkai and Mass Society.* Stanford, Calif.: Stanford University Press, 1970.

Yang, C. K. *Chinese Communist Society: The Family and the Village.* Cambridge, Mass.: M.I.T. Press, 1959.

Index

Abegglen, James C., 50
age group: and international attitudes, 141–46; and party support, 140–41; and views on Constitution, 141; and voting behavior, 81
Ainu, 111
alienation, political, 66, 70, 73
Allison, Graham, 106
Almond, Gabriel, 147
Article 9. *See* Constitution
Asia, familiarity with, by educational level, 150

ban, three, 93n
Benda, Harry J., 130, 133, 134, 135
Bendix, Reinhard, 113
Britain (United Kingdom): middle class of, 99; nation-building in, 113
British Civil Service, 23
Buddhism, 127
bureaucracy, 23–25, 58–60, 96; elite corps of, 20, 24, 59, 60; of France, 24; and LDP and big business, 11, 60; and social scientists, 106
Burks, Ardath W., 111
Burma, 134
business, big: and LDP, 30; and LDP and bureaucracy, 11, 60

Cabinet Secretariat, 25
China: communities of, in Asia, 131, 135; as cultural center, 130; influence of, on Japan, 126, in Asia, 133; Japanese aggression toward, 14, 129; in modern period, 113–14, 115, 119–20; nation-building in, 117, 136; politicocultural system of, 109–10; societies in, 123; views on, by age group, 143, by educational level, 150–51, by party support, 156–57
Ch'in dynasty, 109
Ch'ing dynasty, 110, 112
Chou dynasty, 109
Chūō kōron, 103

Chūritsu-rōren (Chūritsu Rōdō Kumiai Rengō Kaigi), 94n
clientelism, organizational, 11, 13, 56
coalition, 39–40
Confucianism, 127; values of, 126
Conservatives. *See* Liberal Democratic Party
consociational nation, 131
Constitution, 17, 43; Article 9 of, 17, 18, 32, 149; revision of, 11, 18, 94; support of, 19, 32; views on, by age group, 141, by educational level, 147, 149, by party support, 154
consumption, style of, 49
Converse, Philip, 155
Coser, Lewis A., 102
cultural politics, 53, 92, 94, 97, 100n, 154
Curtis, Gerald L., 56

Daalder, Hans, 131, 133
defense policy, views on, by party support, 155, 156. *See also* nuclear armament
Democratic Socialist Party: and Dōmei, 29, 55; organization of, 55; supporters of, 40, 79, 156
Diet, LDP majority in, 12, 14, 23, 58, 59
Dōmei (Zen Nihon Rōdō Sōdōmei), 29, 30, 55
Dore, R. P., 7

East Asia: compared with Europe, 128; cultural uniformity of, 130–31; nation-building in, 121; as region, 124–25
Economic Planning Agency, 23
economy, of Japan, 25–26; international dependency of, 31
Edo (Tokugawa) period, 112
education, 28–29; expansion of higher, 24; level of, and attitudes, 146–47, 149–51; and voting behavior, 80
efficacy, sense of, as variable, 69

167

Kōmei Senkyo Renmei, 34, 56
Korea: Japanese aggression toward, 14, 129, 134; lobby for, 21; in modern period, 113–14, 120; nation-building in, 115–16, 126, 136; participation in, 74–75; pay-off explanation and, 46; politico-cultural system of, 109–10; societies in, 123; stability of, 30; studies on, 124
Korean War, 47
Koryŏ dynasty, 110, 127
Kuwabara Takeo, 113

labor, seasonal, 49
Laborers and Farmers Party, 7
labor unions, 29–30, 89; in Britain and Sweden, 89. *See also* Dōmei, Sōhyō
Latin America, 134, 136
Levy, Marion J., Jr., 113
Liberal Democratic Party: and bureaucracy, 25, 61; and bureaucracy and big business, 11, 60; and Constitution, 17, 19, 94; and Diet majority, 12, 14, 23, 58, 59; foreign policy of, 155; and inflation, 6; and *kōenkai*, 11, 55, 56, 58; and labor unions, 29; and local interests, 21; party structure of, 99; policies of, 21; rule of, 10, 12, 20, 23; supporters of, 8, 53–54, 79, 82, 83, 86, 91, 92–93, 98; traditionalism of, 91
Liberal Party, 6, 18
Lijphart, Arend, 123, 131
Lipset, S. M., 78, 86, 96, 106
local government, *vs.* national government, 60
Lockheed bribery scandal, 3, 10, 13
Lockwood, David, 90

MacArthur, General Douglas, 17
Malaysia, as plural society, 131, 133, 135
manual workers: and party support, 79, 98; voting behavior of, 86, 88
Maruyama Masao, 103, 119
Marx, Karl, 122
Masamura Kimihiro, 5, 6

Massey, Joseph A., 67n
mass media, 26
mass society, traditional, 116
Matsumoto, Yoshiharu Scott, 92
Meiji Restoration, and nation-building, 96, 113n, 118, 120, 121, 123
Meiji state, 119, 122
middle class, urban, 8
Miki Takeo, 13
Ministry of Finance, 23
Ministry of International Trade and Industry, 23, 26, 59
Minobe Ryōkichi, 58
Miyamoto Kenji, 158
Miyazaki Ryūji, 44
mobilization, political, 66, 70, 73–74
Mongolia, studies on, 124
Moore, Barrington, 114
Motoori Norinaga, 127
movements, citizens and residents, 34
multicontextual considerations, 77
multiparty system, 39–40
Myrdal, Gunnar, 125

Nakane Chie, 7, 48
Nara period, 110
nation-building: in East Asia, 121; in Japan, 14, 118–19, 121–23, 126, 128; in Southeast Asia, 125, 129–31, 133–34, 135–36
nations, views on other: by age group, 142–43; by educational level, 149–50; by party support, 158
neighborhood associations, 75
nemawashi, 62
Netherlands, 133
Nie, Norman, 66, 70
Nigeria, 133
northern islands, reversion of, to Japan, 157
Norway, middle class of, 99
nuclear armament, views on: by age group, 144; by educational level, 149

Occupation, of Japan by Allied Forces, 6, 10, 17, 18, 43, 45, 58, 119
occupational groups, voting behav-